MW00686372

MCSE Lab Manual
for Microsoft®
Windows® 2000
Server

Ron Carswell

COURSE
TECHNOLOGY
™
THOMSON LEARNING

Australia • Canada • Mexico • Singapore • Spain • United Kingdom • United States

MCSE Lab Manual for Microsoft Windows 2000 Server is published by Course Technology.

Managing Editor	Stephen Solomon
Senior Product Manager	David George
Production Editor	Debbie Masi
Developmental Editor	Jill Batistick
Quality Assurance Manager	John Bosco
Marketing Manager	Toby Shelton
Text Designer	GEX, Inc.
Composition House	GEX, Inc.
Cover Designer	Joseph Lee, Black Fish Design

Disclaimer

Course Technology reserves the right to revise this publication and make changes from time to time in its content without notice.

The Web addresses in this book are subject to change from time to time as necessary without notice.

For more information, contact Course Technology, 25 Thomson Pace, Boston, MA 02210;

or find us on the World Wide Web at *www.course.com*.

For permission to use material from this text or product, contact us by

- Web: www.thomsonrights.com
- Phone: 1-800-730-2214
- Fax: 1-800-730-2215

ISBN 0-619-01516-0

Printed in Canada

3 4 5 WC 04 03 02

TABLE OF CONTENTS

INTRODUCTION

The objective of this lab manual is to assist you in preparing for the Microsoft certification exam # 70-215: *Installing, Configuring, and Administering Microsoft Windows 2000 Server* by applying the Windows 2000 Server exam objectives to relevant lab activities. This text is designed to be used in conjunction with *MCSE Guide to Microsoft Windows 2000 Server* (0-619-01517-9), but it also can be used to supplement any MCSE courseware. Although this manual is written with the intent of it being used in a classroom lab environment, it also may be used for self-study on a home network.

FEATURES

In order to ensure a successful experience for instructors and students alike, this book includes the following features:

- **Microsoft Windows 2000 Server MCSE Certification objectives** — For each chapter, the relevant objectives from MCSE Exam # 70-215 are listed

- **Lab Objectives** — Every lab has a brief description and list of learning objectives

- **Completion Times** — Every lab has an estimated completion time so that you can plan your activities more accurately

- **Activity Sections** — Labs are presented in manageable sections

- **Step-by-step instructions** — Provide steps to enhance technical proficiency

- **Review questions** — Help reinforce concepts presented in the lab

HARDWARE REQUIREMENTS

- A Pentium 200 MHz CPU or higher

- 128 MB of RAM

- A 2GB hard disk with at least 1GB of storage

- An optional second disk drive with at least 1GB MB of storage

- A modem

- A CD-ROM drive

- A network interface card connected to a cable system

NETWORK REQUIREMENTS

- A Windows 2000 Server participating as a domain controller for the lonestar.com domain

- Optionally, for home use, a Small Office Home Office (SOHO) kit consisting of two Ethernet cards, an Ethernet hub or switch, and category 5 data cables

SOFTWARE/SETUP REQUIREMENTS

- Access to a Windows 2000 Server CD

- Access to a Windows 2000 Server Resource kit CD

- Windows 2000 Server installed in the primary partition with at least 1GB of storage space. (If a partition other than the primary partition is selected, adjust the drive references in the labs to reflect this choice.)

- At least 100 MB of free space on an extended disk partition

- A personal computer with no existing operating system (In order to perform the installation from the installation disks in chapter 5, the drive should have no less than 2GB of free storage)

- A modem and a modem line. (If necessary, a telco line simulator could be used to facilitate the modem line and PBX, or you could use a null modem cable.)

CHAPTER ONE

NETWORKING WITH MICROSOFT WINDOWS 2000

Labs included in this chapter

➤ Lab 1.1 Plan for an Office Server Network Installation

➤ Lab 1.2 Plan for a Domain Server Network Installation

➤ Lab 1.3 Discover Windows 2000 Server Resource Sharing Capabilities

➤ Lab 1.4 Summarize File System Compatibilities

➤ Lab 1.5 Monitor System Activity with the Task Manager

Microsoft MCSE Exam #70-215 Objectives

Objective	Lab
Perform an attended installation of Windows 2000	1.1, 1.2, 1.4
Perform an unattended installation of Windows 2000 Server	1.1, 1.2
Upgrade a server from Windows NT 4.0	1.2, 1.4
Monitor, configure, troubleshoot and control access to files, folders, and shared folders	1.1, 1.2, 1.3
Configure hardware devices	1.1, 1.2
Monitor and optimize usage of system resources	1.5
Manage processes	1.5
Monitor, configure and troubleshoot disks and volumes	1.4

LAB 1.1 PLAN FOR AN OFFICE SERVER NETWORK INSTALLATION

Objectives

The goal of this lab is to plan for a small network of personal computers, including a central workgroup file/print server. Names identify computers and shared resources. The typical small network uses Ethernet topology with a shared hub and category 5 (CAT 5) cabling. As a network administrator, you will plan for the networking of personal computers. After completing this lab, you will be able to:

➤ Develop a network diagram with a file/print server

➤ Specify computer names

Materials Required

This lab will require the following:

➤ Access to MCSE Guide to Windows 2000 Server for each student

➤ A drawing program is optional.

Activity Background

TexStar experienced rapid sales growth for imprinted shirts and caps. After three years of operation, TexStar acquired several personal computers. Table 1-1 lists the current TexStar computer inventory.

TexStar installed modular furniture, which provides cable ways for data and voice, and an isolated conduit for electrical power. TexStar wants to install a workgroup file/print server to share file and printer resources. TexStar owns a 12-page-per-minute (ppm) laser printer and a 6-ppm laser printer. In addition to the existing printers, TexStar purchased an 8-ppm color laser printer and a 24-ppm laser printer. Multiple employees will use all printers.

TexStar wants to upgrade the existing network to include a file/print server. You will prepare technical documents for the owner/manager of TexStar. You will need a computer name for the server and a network diagram.

Table 1-1   TexStar Computers After Three Years

Computer	Job Title	Processor	Operating System	Memory	Hard Drive
Owner	Owner/Manager	PIII 650	Windows 2000 Professional	128 MB	20 GB
Reception01	Receptionist	P233MMX	Windows 95	64 MB	4 GB
Sales01	Sales	PII 333	Windows 98	64 MB	6.4 GB
Sales02	Sales	PIII 650	Windows 2000 Professional	128 MB	20 GB
Sales03	Sales	PIII 650	Windows 2000 Professional	128 MB	20 GB
Account01	Accountant	PIII 500	Windows 98	128 MB	10 GB
Account02	Accountant	PIII 650	Windows 2000 Professional	128 MB	20 GB
Payroll01	Payroll	PIII 650	Windows 2000 Professional	128 MB	20 GB
Purchase01	Purchasing	PII 350	Windows 98	64 MB	10 GB
Purchase02	Purchasing	PIII 650	Windows 2000 Professional	128 MB	20 GB
Traffic01	Traffic Control	PIII 650	Windows 2000 Professional	128 MB	20 GB

Estimated completion time: **30 minutes**

ACTIVITY

1. Specify a computer name for the workgroup file/print server.

   _____

2. Draw a network diagram for your revised network. Include the names of computers.

   _____

   _____

   _____

   _____

   _____

   _____

   _____

   _____

   _____

Certification Objectives

Objectives for Microsoft Exam 70-215: Installing, Configuring, and Administering Microsoft®
Windows® 2000 Server:

➤ Perform an attended installation of Windows 2000

➤ Perform an unattended installation of Windows 2000

➤ Configure hardware devices

Review Questions

1. Which of the following operating systems supports file and printer sharing with
   centralized account management?
   a. Windows 2000 Professional
   b. Windows 2000 Server
   c. Windows 95
   d. Windows NT 4.0 Server
   e. Windows 98

2. Users connected to a central file/print server can access which of the following
   shared resources from the central file/print server?
   a. subdirectories located on disk drives for the central server
   b. applications, such as word processors, stored on the central server
   c. printers on the local workstations
   d. printers on the central server
   e. processors on the central server

3. Which of the following is an advantage that a central file/print server network
   has over a peer-to-peer network?
   a. centralized management of passwords for shared resources
   b. centralized backup for critical files
   c. network support for over 10 users
   d. auditing access to sensitive files

4. Sharing resources within a peer-to-peer network requires a password for each
   shared resource. Passwords are stored on the personal computer that provides the
   shared resource. Which of the following is a problem with peer-to-peer password
   protection?
   a. Users must remember multiple passwords.
   b. Password changes must be communicated to all resource users.
   c. Shares are implemented with passwords that are identical to the share name.
   d. Decentralized passwords are easier to implement than centralized passwords.
   e. Users record passwords as notes at their desks.

Lab 1.2 Plan for a Domain Server Network Installation

Objectives

The goal of this lab is to plan for a network of personal computers, including a domain controller. When your office network expands to include multiple file/print servers, a domain controller is added. The domain controller maintains user accounts for the domain. In addition, the domain controller provides file/print resources. After completing this lab, you will be able to:

➤ Develop a network diagram with a domain controller

➤ Specify computer and resource names

Materials Required

This lab will require the following:

➤ Access to *MCSE Guide to Windows 2000 Server* for each student

➤ A drawing program is optional.

Activity Background

TexStar experienced continued sales growth for imprinted shirts and caps. Table 1-2 lists the computer configuration within the company after four years.

Table 1-2   TexStar Computers After Four Years

Computer	Job Title	Processor	Operating System	Memory	Hard Drive
Server01	File/Print Server	PIII 850	Windows 2000 Server	256 MB	128 GB
Owner	Owner/Manager	PIII 650	Windows 2000 Professional	128 MB	20 GB
Secretary01	Secretary	PIII 800	Windows 2000 Professional	128 MB	20 GB
Reception01	Receptionist	PIII 650	Windows 2000 Professional	128 MB	20 GB
Sales04	Sales Manager	PIII 800	Windows 2000 Professional	128 MB	20 GB
Sales01	Sales	PIII 650	Windows 2000 Professional	128 MB	20 GB
Sales02	Sales	PIII 650	Windows 2000 Professional	128 MB	20 GB
Sales03	Sales	PIII 650	Windows 2000 Professional	128 MB	20 GB
Sales05	Sales	PIII 800	Windows 2000 Professional	128 MB	20 GB

Table 1-2   TexStar Computers After Four Years (continued)

Computer	Job Title	Processor	Operating System	Memory	Hard Drive
Sales06	Sales	PIII 800	Windows 2000 Professional	128 MB	20 GB
Account01	Accountant	PIII 500	Windows 98	128 MB	10 GB
Account02	Accountant	PIII 650	Windows 2000 Professional	128 MB	20 GB
Account03	Accountant	PIII 800	Windows 2000 Professional	128 MB	20 GB
Payroll01	Payroll	PIII 650	Windows 2000 Professional	128 MB	20 GB
Purchase01	Purchasing	PIII 650	Windows 2000 Professional	128 MB	20 GB
Purchase02	Purchasing	PIII 650	Windows 2000 Professional	128 MB	20 GB
Purchase03	Purchasing	PIII 800	Windows 2000 Professional	128 MB	20 GB
Traffic01	Traffic Control	PIII 650	Windows 2000 Professional	128 MB	20 GB
Traffic02	Traffic Control	PIII 800	Windows 2000 Professional	128 MB	20 GB

TexStar retained the modular furniture that provides cable ways for data and voice and an isolated conduit for electrical power. Now the company wants to add an additional server.

Estimated completion time: **30 minutes**

ACTIVITY

1. Specify a domain name and a computer name for the new server.

   _____

2. Draw a network diagram for your proposed network. Include the names of computers.

   _____

   _____

   _____

   _____

   _____

Certification Objectives

Objectives for Microsoft Exam 70-215: Installing, Configuring, and Administering Microsoft®
Windows® 2000 Server:

➤ Perform an attended installation of Windows 2000

➤ Perform an unattended installation of Windows 2000

➤ Upgrade a server from Microsoft Windows NT 4.0

➤ Configure hardware devices

➤ Monitor, configure, troubleshoot, and control local security on files and folders

➤ Monitor, configure, troubleshoot, and control access to files, folders, and shared
folders

Review Questions

1. Which of the following operating systems supports domain-wide centralized
account management?
   a. Windows 2000 Professional
   b. Windows 2000 Server
   c. Windows 95
   d. Windows NT 4.0 Server
   e. Windows 98

2. The ABC Company wants to enhance the existing network by installing a
Windows 2000 Server. The current network consists of a Windows 2000
file/print server for the storage of critical company documents. Twenty-two personal computers with Windows 2000 Professional installed are connected to the
file/print server. The existing file/print server supports four printers. ABC
Company contracts with XYZ Company to update the network.

   George from the ABC Company recommends the following:
   ■ Implement a Windows 2000 Server domain controller.
   ■ Migrate approximately 40 percent of the user data to the new domain
   controller.
   ■ Retain the local user accounts on the file/print server for ease of use.
   ■ Reallocate the printers between the servers.
   Required Objective
   ■ Implement centralized account management for users and resources.
   Optional Objectives
   ■ Balance data resources between the two servers
   ■ Balance printers between the two servers

3. Which of the following statements regarding the solution proposed by George is true?

   a. meets the required objective and no optional objectives

   b. meets the required objective and one optional objective

   c. meets the required objective and two optional objectives

   d. does not meet the required objective

LAB 1.3 DISCOVER WINDOWS 2000 SERVER RESOURCE SHARING CAPABILITIES

Objectives

The goal of this lab is to discover Windows 2000 Server resource sharing capabilities. You will locate files and printers that are shared resources. After completing this lab, you will be able to use the Explorer application to:

➤ Locate a server on the network

➤ Determine the resources that the server shares

➤ Determine access permissions to the shared resources

Materials Required

This lab will require the following:

➤ Access to a personal computer running Windows 2000 Professional or Windows 2000 Server

➤ A valid user domain account and password

➤ The name of a server that permits access to file and printer resources

Estimated completion time: **30 minutes**

ACTIVITY

1. To access a resource on a remote computer, log on to the provided computer by pressing **Ctrl+Alt+Delete**. Enter the supplied user name and password. (You may need to select a domain name.)

2. Click the **Start** button, click **Run**, type **explorer** in the text box, and then click **OK**.

3. Expand **My Network Places** in the left pane.

Click on the + to expand an item in the left pane. Click on the – to collapse an item.

1

4. Expand **Entire Network** in the left pane, then expand **Microsoft Windows Network** in the left pane.

5. Expand *domain* (where *domain* is the domain to which the server is attached), and then double-click the *server name* provided by your instructor.

6. Double-click a folder in the right pane. Observe the shared subdirectories and files.

7. Right-click in the white space in the right pane, and then click **Properties**. Click the **Security** tab. Observe and record the permissions for the shared subdirectory. Click **Cancel** and then click the **Back** button.

8. Double-click the **Printers** folder. Observe the shared printers.

9. Click the **Close** button to close Explorer.

Certification Objectives

Objectives for Microsoft Exam 70-215: Installing, Configuring, and Administering Microsoft® Windows® 2000 Server:

➤ Monitor, configure, troubleshoot, and control access to files, folders, and shared folders

➤ Monitor, configure, troubleshoot, and control local security on files and folders

Review Questions

1. What are the correct file/directory share permissions for Windows 2000 Server?
   a. No Control
   b. Read
   c. Write
   d. Full Control
   e. Change

2. Which resource type can be shared by Windows 2000 Server?
   a. files
   b. serial ports
   c. printers
   d. subdirectories
   e. parallel ports

LAB 1.4 SUMMARIZE FILE SYSTEM COMPATIBILITIES

Objectives

The goal of this lab is to summarize file system compatibilities for Windows 2000 Server and other operating systems. You will complete a file system compatibility table. After completing this lab, you will be able to:

➤ List the characteristics for supported file systems

➤ Determine potential file system incompatibilities for various operating systems

Materials Required

This lab will require the following:

➤ Access to the *MCSE Guide to Windows 2000 Server*

Estimated completion time: **30 minutes**

ACTIVITY

1. Complete Table 1-3.

Table 1-3   File System Compatibilities for Operating Systems Installation

Feature	FAT16	FAT32	NTFS	CDFS	UDF
Total Volume Size					
Removable Volumes					
Read/Write					
File Security					
File Compression					
Fault Tolerance					
Windows 95/98/ME					
Windows NT 4.0					
Windows 2000					

2. Supply the appropriate Windows operating systems for each file system.
   1. FAT16 _____
   2. FAT32 _____
   3. NTFS _____
   4. CDFS _____
   5. UDF _____

Certification Objectives

Objectives for Microsoft Exam 70-215: Installing, Configuring, and Administering Microsoft® Windows® 2000 Server:

➤ Perform an attended installation of Windows 2000

➤ Upgrade a server from Windows NT 4.0

➤ Monitor, configure, troubleshoot, disks and volumes

Review Questions

1. Windows 2000 Server supports which of the following native file systems?
   a. FAT16
   b. NFS
   c. NTFS
   d. CDFS
   e. UDF
   f. FAT32

2. Which of the following operating systems supports FAT32?
   a. Windows 98
   b. Windows ME
   c. Windows NT 4.0
   d. Windows 2000 Professional
   e. Windows 2000 Server

LAB 1.5 MONITOR SYSTEM ACTIVITY WITH THE TASK MANAGER

Objectives

The goal of this lab is to monitor system activity with the Task Manager. You will view graphs of current system utilization. You will start a program and observe the changes in system utilization. You will terminate this program with the Task Manager. The monitoring of system activity is crucial to the health of your servers. After completing this lab, you will be able to:

➤ View system activity with the Task Manager

➤ Start a program with the Task Manager

➤ Locate a specific running program

➤ Terminate the running program

Materials Required

This lab will require the following:

➤ Access to a personal computer running Windows 2000 Professional or Windows 2000 Server

➤ A valid user domain account and password

Estimated completion time: **30 minutes**

ACTIVITY

1. If necessary, log on to the provided computer by pressing **Ctrl+Alt+Delete**. Enter the supplied user name and password. (You may need to select a domain name.)

2. Right-click the **taskbar** (*Hint:* The taskbar contains the Start button.)

3. Click **Task Manager**.

4. Click the **Performance** tab. Observe and record the CPU usage.

   To simulate activity, move the Windows Task Manager window. Observe the CPU usage and the changes to CPU usage history.

5. Observe and record the MEM usage. Click the **File** menu. Click **New Task (run...)**. Click in the **Open** text box, type **notepad**, and then click **OK**. Observe the changes to the MEM usage and the memory usage history.

6. Click the **Applications** tab in the Windows Task Manager dialog box. Locate and click "**Untitled – Notepad**". Click the **End Task** button to stop the Notepad application.

7. **Close** the Task Manager.

Certification Objectives

Objectives for Microsoft Exam 70-215: Installing, Configuring, and Administering Microsoft® Windows® 2000 Server:

➤ Monitor and optimize usage of system resources

➤ Manage processes

➤ Set priorities and start and stop processes

Review Questions

1. The Task Manager dialog box contains which of the following tabs?
   a. Applications
   b. Programs
   c. Threads
   d. Processes
   e. Performance

2. Which of the following pieces of information can you find on the Performance tab of the Task Manager dialog box?
   a. process usage in percentages
   b. CPU usage in percentages
   c. CPU usage as a line graph
   d. handle usage in percentages
   e. physical memory usage in kilobytes

3. You suspect that your personal computer has performance problems. You monitor your system with the Task Manager. You observe that the memory usage varies as you run additional applications. The MEM usage indicates that you consistently have usage above 80 percent. What action should you take to alleviate your problem?
   a. Return the personal computer to the dealer.
   b. Install a faster processor.
   c. Run the Windows 2000 Disk Optimizer.
   d. Purchase additional memory.
   e. Install a second hard drive.

CHAPTER TWO

PLANNING FOR SERVER HARDWARE

Labs included in this chapter

➤ Lab 2.1 Determine Hardware Configuration with Dianostic Program

➤ Lab 2.2 Utilize Hardware Compatibility List

➤ Lab 2.3 View Available Disk Space

➤ Lab 2.4 Investigate RAID Approaches

➤ Lab 2.5 Calculate Data Capacities

Microsoft MCSE Exam #70-215 Objectives	
Objective	**Lab**
Perform an attended installation of Windows 2000	2.1, 2.2, 2.3
Perform an unattended installation of Windows 2000 Server	2.1, 2.2, 2.3
Upgrade a server from Windows NT 4.0	2.2
Troubleshoot failed installations	2.1, 2.2
Configure hardware devices	2.1, 2.2
Troubleshoot problems with hardware	2.1, 2.2
Optimize disk performance	2.4, 2.5
Manage and optimize availability of system state data and user data	2.4, 2.5
Recover systems and user data	2.4, 2.5
Monitor, configure, and troubleshoot disks and volumes	2.4, 2.5
Recover from disk failures	2.4, 2.5
Install, configure, and troubleshoot network adapters and drivers	2.1, 2.2

LAB 2.1 DETERMINE HARDWARE CONFIGURATION WITH DIAGNOSTIC PROGRAM

Objectives

The goal of this lab is to determine the hardware of one or more computers on which you plan to install Windows 2000 Server. You must determine if the personal computers meet the minimum requirements to install Windows 2000 Server. In the next lab, the recorded information will be checked against the Microsoft Hardware Compatibility List. After completing this lab, you will be able to:

➤ Run a Windows operating system diagnostic program

➤ Determine the installed hardware for a personal computer

➤ Develop a hardware list

Materials Required

This lab will require the following:

➤ Access to a computer with a Microsoft Windows product (Windows 95 or 98, Windows NT 4.0, or Windows 2000)

➤ Access to *MCSE Guide to Windows 2000 Server* for each student.

Estimated completion time: **30 minutes**

ACTIVITY

1. If you are using a personal computer with Windows NT 4.0, do the following, and then go to Step 4:

    a. Click the **Start** button on the taskbar.

    b. Point to **Programs**, point to **Administrative Tools (Common)**, and then click **Windows NT Diagnostics**.

    c. Click and then view the contents of these tabs: **Version**, **System**, **Display**, **Drives**, and **Memory**.

    d. **Close** the Windows NT Diagnostics window.

    e. Click the **Start** button on the taskbar, point to **Settings**, and then click **Control Panel**.

    f. Double-click the **Network** icon, and then click the **Adapters** tab. Record the information in Step 4.

    g. **Close** the Network window.

    h. Double-click the **SCSI Adapters** icon. Record the information in Step 4.

    i. **Close** the SCSI Adapters window.

    j. **Close** the Control Panel window.

2

2. If you are using a personal computer with Windows 95 or 98, do the following, and then go to Step 4:
   a. Right-click the **My Computer** desktop icon.
   b. Click **Properties**.
   c. Click the **Device Manager** tab.

 Click on the + to expand an entry in the Device Manager. Click on the – to collapse an entry.

3. If you are using a personal computer with Windows 2000, do the following, and then go to Step 4:
   a. Right-click the **My Computer** desktop icon.
   b. Click **Properties**.
   c. Click the **Hardware** tab.
   d. Click the **Device Manager** command button.

4. Determine the following information about your computer:
   Processor type ———————————————————————————
   Disk drive(s) ————————————————————————————
   Disk drive controller(s) ——————————————————————
   Display adapter ————————————————————————————
   Display monitor ————————————————————————————
   DVD/CD-ROM drive(s) ——————————————————————
   Network adapter(s) ———————————————————————

5. **Close** open windows.

Certification Objectives

Objectives for Microsoft Exam 70-215: Installing, Configuring, and Administering Microsoft®
Windows® 2000 Server:

➤ Perform an attended installation of Windows 2000

➤ Perform an unattended installation of Windows 2000

➤ Configure hardware devices

➤ Troubleshoot problems with hardware

Review Questions

1. What's the best way to find out which devices are being used on a Windows 2000 server?
   a. Device Manager
   b. System Monitor

    c. Windows 2000 Hardware Qualifier

    d. IRQ Monitor

2. When preparing for a Windows 2000 Server installation, identification of hardware devices is critical to the success of the installation. Which devices are critical to the installation?

    a. processor type

    b. disk drive(s)

    c. CD-ROM drive

    d. Zip drive

    e. display adapter

    f. network adapters(s)

    g. disk drive controller(s)

LAB 2.2 UTILIZE HARDWARE COMPATIBILITY LIST

Objectives

The goal of this lab is to review the hardware for one or more computers on which you plan to install Windows 2000 Server. In the previous lab, you developed a hardware list for the personal computers that you are considering for an installation of Windows 2000 Server. Before attempting the installation, you will want to check your hardware against the Hardware Compatibility List (HCL) at the Microsoft Web site. The Microsoft Logo program provides information about the availability of software drivers for each hardware item. After completing this lab, you will be able to:

➤ Connect to the Microsoft Web site

➤ Locate the Hardware Compatibility List (HCL)

➤ Verify that hardware in Lab 2.1 conforms to the HCL

➤ Review the Microsoft Logo program

Materials Required

This lab will require the following:

➤ Access to www.microsoft.com for each student

➤ Access to *MCSE Guide to Windows 2000 Server* for each student

Estimated completion time: **30 minutes**

ACTIVITY

1. Start **Microsoft Internet Explorer**. Type **www.microsoft.com/hcl/** in the Address box, and then press **Enter**.

2. Go to **Lab 2.1**, and note the **processor type** that you entered. Enter that text into the "Search for the following" text box, and then click **go**.

If you receive "no results that match your query," reformulate your query and enter it again.

3. Repeat Step 2 for the remaining pieces of information that you listed in Lab 2.1.

4. Click the **legend** link on the results page. Review the **Legend** window. Write the Microsoft Logo categories on the following lines: _____

_____

_____

_____

_____

5. If your research reveals hardware incompatibilities, review the information with your instructor. He or she might have a workaround. Close Internet Explorer.

Certification Objectives

Objectives for Microsoft Exam 70-215: Installing, Configuring, and Administering Microsoft® Windows® 2000 Server:

➤ Perform an attended installation of Windows 2000

➤ Perform an unattended installation of Windows 2000

➤ Configure hardware devices

➤ Troubleshoot problems with hardware

Review Questions

1. Microsoft established the Logo program to classify hardware product compatibility for Windows 2000. Which of the following is a classification in the Logo program?

   a. Product meets all requirements.

   b. Product requires a driver to be downloaded.

   c. Product has driver on the Windows Operating System CD.

   d. Product does not meet requirements.

   e. Product has been deemed compatible with Windows.

2. Which items are required for the installation of Windows 2000 Server?
   a. pointing device
   b. 685 MB available on hard disk
   c. Pentium 133 or better processor
   d. VGA video adapter
   e. VGA monitor
   f. serial port
   g. parallel port
   h. USB port
   i. CD-ROM
   j. 64 MB of RAM (minimum)
   k. level-2 memory cache
   l. network interface card

LAB 2.3 VIEW AVAILABLE DISK SPACE

Objectives

The goal of this lab is to determine the available disk space for the installation of Windows 2000 Server. If your selected personal computer does not meet the free disk space requirements of 685 MB, you will not be able to complete the installation of Windows 2000 Server. After completing this lab exercise, you will be able to:

➤ Use various tools to determine the available disk space on a hard disk

Materials Required

This lab will require the following:

➤ Access to a computer with a Microsoft Windows product (Windows 95 or 98, Windows NT 4.0, or Windows 2000)

➤ Access to *MCSE Guide to Windows 2000 Server* for each student

Estimated completion time: **30 minutes**

ACTIVITY

1. If you are using a personal computer with Windows 95 or 98, do the following, and then go to Step 4:
   a. Double-click the **My Computer** desktop icon.
   b. Right-click each local hard drive.
   c. Click **Properties** and review the free space for each local hard drive.

2

2. If you are using a personal computer with Windows NT 4.0, do the following, and then go to Step 4:

   a. Click the **Start** button on the taskbar.

   b. Point to **Programs**, point to **Administrative Tools (Common)**, and then click **Disk Administrator**.

   c. Right-click each local drive, click **Properties**, and then review the free space for each local hard drive.

3. If you are using a personal computer with Windows 2000, do the following, and then go to Step 4:

   a. Click the **Start** button on the taskbar.

   b. Point to **Programs**, point to **Administrative Tools**, and then click **Computer Management**.

   c. Expand **Storage**, and then click **Disk Management**.

   d. Right-click each local drive, click **Properties**, and then observe the free space on the local drives.

4. Complete Table 2-1.

Table 2-1   Free Space on Your Computer

Disk	Drive Letters	Free Space

5. **Close** all open windows.

Certification Objectives

Objectives for Microsoft Exam 70-215: Installing, Configuring, and Administering Microsoft® Windows® 2000 Server:

➤ Perform an attended installation of Windows 2000

➤ Perform an unattended installation of Windows 2000

Review Questions

1. What is the minimum hard disk space for the installation of Windows 2000 Server?

   a. 130 MB

   b. 512 MB

   c. 685 MB

   d. 1,200 MB

   e. 2,400 MB

LAB 2.4 INVESTIGATE RAID APPROACHES

Objectives

The goal of this lab is to investigate the Windows 2000 Server software RAID options. As a network administrator, you will evaluate the need for the various RAID implementations for your servers. After completing this lab exercise, you will be able to:

➤ Launch Windows 2000 Help

➤ Research the RAID options of Windows 2000 Server

Materials Required

This lab will require the following:

➤ Access to a computer with Microsoft Windows 2000 Server

➤ Access to *MCSE Guide to Windows 2000 Server* for each student

Estimated completion time: **30 minutes**

ACTIVITY

1. Click **Start**, and then click **Help**. If necessary, click the **Show** icon to display the tabs for Contents, Index, and Search.

2. Click the **Search** tab, type **using mirrored volumes** in the Type in the word(s) to search for text box, and then click **List Topics**.

3. Click **Using mirrored volumes** under Select topic, and then click **Display**.

4. Read the information regarding mirrored volumes.

5. Type **using RAID-5 volumes** in the Type in the word(s) to search for text box, and then click **List Topics**.

6. Click **Using RAID-5 volumes** under Select topic, and then click **Display**.

7. Read the information regarding RAID-5 volumes.

8. Type **using striped volumes** in the Type in the word(s) to search for text box, and then click **List Topics**.

9. Click **Using striped volumes** under Select topic, and then click **Display**.

10. Read the information regarding striped volumes.

11. Close the **Help** window.

Certification Objectives

Objectives for Microsoft Exam 70-215: Installing, Configuring, and Administering Microsoft® Windows® 2000 Server:

➤ disk performance

➤ Manage and optimize availability of system state data and user data.

➤ Recover systems and user data

➤ Monitor, configure, and troubleshoot disks and volumes

➤ Recover from disk failures

Review Questions

1. Two hard disks is the minimum hardware requirement for which of the following RAID options?
   a. disk striping without parity
   b. volume sets
   c. disk mirroring
   d. disk duplexing

2. You want to implement a fault tolerant strategy for your data files on a Windows 2000 server with three hard disks and one controller. System and boot files are on another independent disk. You want to optimize storage space. Which of the following would you use?
   a. disk striping
   b. disk duplexing
   c. disk mirroring
   d. disk striping with parity

3. A1 Company wants to implement a Windows 2000 server for the storage of critical company data. They contact John, a consultant, to obtain his recommendations.

   Required objective:
   ■ A1 requires redundancy for the operating system

   Optional objectives:
   ■ Databases must be available for 18 hours each day
   ■ Databases must be available even when one disk drive is not available

   John, the consultant, recommends a SCSI adapter with 6 data disks of 9 GB each. John contends that a RAID-5 will meet all of the requirements. You are asked to review John's solution against the requirements. What do you tell your boss about the solution?
   a. meets the required objective and no optional objectives
   b. meets the required objective and one optional objective
   c. meets the required objective and two optional objectives
   d. does not meet the required objective

4. Brian and Lillie are discussing the merits of RAID-0 and RAID-5. Brian contends that RAID-0 provides the best file performance. Lillie points out that RAID-5 provides data protection. You are asked to moderate the discussion. What do you say to Brian and Lillie?

a. RAID-0 does not provide fault tolerance.

b. RAID-0 does provide fault tolerance.

c. RAID-5 provides fault tolerance with reasonable file performance.

d. RAID-5 does not provide fault tolerance.

e. RAID-1 should be considered for redundant storage of the operating system.

LAB 2.5 CALCULATE DATA CAPACITIES

Objectives

The goal of this lab is to calculate available data storage for various software RAID configurations. As a network administrator, you must allocate free space to create the various RAID implementations. The amount of free space on multiple hard drives dictates the size of the RAID that can be configured. After completing this lab exercise, you will be able to:

➤ Calculate the approximate storage capacities of software RAID alternatives

➤ Indicate the volume allocations for the various software RAID alternatives

Materials Required

This lab will require the following:

➤ Access to *MCSE Guide to Windows 2000 Server* for each student

Estimated completion time: **30 minutes**

ACTIVITY

1. One fault-tolerant option for server operating systems is to use disk mirroring (RAID-1) to store redundant data. With disk mirroring, the data is copied by the operating system from the first drive to the second drive. The area for the secondary allocation is the same size as the primary allocation. For the available free disk space depicted in Table 2-2, indicate the maximum amount of redundant data that could be stored using disk mirroring.

Table 2-2 Available Raw Disk Space

Disk 0	Disk 1
Allocated 2 GB Free Space = 6.4 GB	Free Space = 8.4 GB
Maximum amount of data in Disk 0 would be:	Maximum amount of data in Disk 1 would be:

The maximum amount of data stored would be _____.

2. For fast access to data, you could implement RAID-0 or striped volumes. Data access for striped volumes is fast because the data is divided into equal blocks where the blocks are quickly accessed through multiple disk reads and data paths. Because the blocks are evenly spread across multiple disks, an equivalent amount of disk space must be allocated on each drive. The raw disk space would be allocated with Windows 2000 Disk Management. For the available free disk space depicted in Table 2-3, indicate the maximum amount of data that could be stored using RAID-0.

Table 2-3   Available Raw Disk Space

Disk 1	Disk 2	Disk 3	Disk 4	Disk 5
Unpartitioned disk space: 4 GB	Unpartitioned disk space: 5 GB	Unpartitioned disk space: 4.2 GB	Unpartitioned disk space: 4.8 GB	Unpartitioned disk space: 16 GB
Maximum amount of data:	Maximum amount of data:	Maximum amount of data:	Maximum amount of data:	Maximum amount of data:

The maximum amount of data stored would be _____.

3. For fast access to data protected by data redundancy, you could implement RAID-5. Because the data and parity blocks are evenly spread across multiple disks, an equivalent amount of disk space must be allocated on each drive. Include one additional disk allocation for the parity information. The raw disk space would be allocated with Windows 2000 Disk Management. For the available unpartitioned disk space depicted in Table 2-4, indicate the maximum amount of data that could be stored using RAID-5.

Table 2-4   Available Raw Disk Space to Allocate for RAID-5

Disk 1	Disk 2	Disk 3	Disk 4	Disk 5
Unpartitioned disk space: 4 GB	Unpartitioned disk space: 5 GB	Unpartitioned disk space: 4.2 GB	Unpartitioned disk space: 4.8 GB	Unpartitioned disk space: 16 GB
Maximum amount of data:	Maximum amount of data:	Maximum amount of data:	Maximum amount of data:	Maximum amount of data:

The maximum amount of data stored would be _____.

Certification Objectives

Objectives for Microsoft Exam 70-215:Installing, Configuring, and Administering Microsoft®
Windows® 2000 Server:

➤ Optimize disk performance

➤ Manage and optimize availability of system state data and user data

➤ Recover system and user data

➤ Monitor, configure, and troubleshoot disks and volumes

➤ Recover from disk failures

Review Questions

1. You have five hard disks on your computer. The first disk contains the boot and
   system files. The remaining four disks have 1.2 GB, 2 GB, 2.1 GB, and 2.4 GB of
   raw space, respectively. How much disk space is available for the storage of data if
   you create the largest possible RAID-5?

   a. 3.6 GB

   b. 4 GB

   c. 4.8 GB

   d. 6 GB

   e. 6.5 GB

2. You have two hard disks on your computer. The first disk contains the boot and
   system files, which require 1.2 GB of space. In addition, you have 2 GB of data
   on the first disk. The second disk has 3.2 GB of raw space. You mirror the first
   disk on the second disk. How much disk space is available for the storage of data
   within the mirror set?

   a. 1.2 GB

   b. 2 GB

   c. 3.2 GB

   d. 5.2 GB

   e. 6.4 GB

3. You have five hard disks on your computer. The first disk contains the boot and
   system files, which require 1.2 GB of space. The five disks have 1.2 GB, 3.2 GB,
   2 GB, 2.1 GB, and 2.4 GB of raw space, respectively. You mirror the boot and
   system files on the second disk. How much disk space is available for the storage
   of data if you create the largest possible RAID-5 with the remaining disk space?

   a. 4.8 GB

   b. 6 GB

   c. 8 GB

   d. 8.5 GB

   e. 9.7 GB

PLANNING NETWORK PROTOCOLS AND COMPATIBILITY

Labs included in this chapter

➤ Lab 3.1 Determine Windows 2000 IP Configuration

➤ Lab 3.2 Determine TCP/IP Connectivity

➤ Lab 3.3 Review IP Addressing

➤ Lab 3.4 Install and Remove the NetBEUI Protocol (Optional Lab)

➤ Lab 3.5 Investigate Network Protocols

Microsoft MCSE Exam #70-215 Objectives	
Objective	Lab
Install and configure network services for interoperability	3.1, 3.2, 3.3 3.5
Configure driver signing options	3.1
Update device drivers	3.1
Install, configure, and troubleshoot network protocols	3.1, 3.2, 3.3 3.4, 3.5
Install and configure network services	3.1
Configure the properties of a connection	3.1, 3.2
Install, configure, and troubleshoot network adapters and drivers	3.1

LAB 3.1 DETERMINE WINDOWS 2000 IP CONFIGURATION

Objectives

The goal of this lab is to determine the IP configuration of a personal computer with Windows 2000 Server. (The IP configuration could also be determined on a computer with Windows 2000 Professional.) The information that you collect in this lab will be needed for the next lab.

Recall that for a personal computer to communicate with other personal computers on an IP network, a unique IP address and a subnet mask are required. Also, the gateway address must be specified to communicate with a personal computer on a remote segment. After completing this lab, you will be able to:

➤ Run the ipconfig diagnostic program

➤ Determine the IP configuration for a personal computer

➤ Determine the IP configuration for a network adapter

➤ Use the more command to display console output one page at a time

Materials Required

This lab will require the following:

➤ Access to a computer with Windows 2000 Server or Professional with the TCP/IP protocol installed

Estimated completion time: **30 minutes**

ACTIVITY

1. Start your computer and wait until the desktop is visible. Click **Start**, point to **Programs**, point to **Accessories**, and then click **Command Prompt**.

2. At the command prompt, type **ipconfig /all | more**, and then press **Enter**.

The pipe character "|," which is located above the Enter key on your keyboard, redirects the console output to the more command. To view additional pages when piping the output to the more command, press the Space Bar.

3. Record the following information about the Windows 2000 IP configuration:
   Host name: _____
   (This is the host name for the personal computer.)

4. Record the following about the network adapter, and then leave the command-prompt window open for the next activity:

Connection-specific DNS suffix: _____

(This is the internetwork suffix for your host.)

Description: _____

  (This is the description for the network adapter.)

  Physical address: _____

  (This is the MAC or hardware address for the adapter.)

  IP address: _____

  (This is the address of the personal computer.)

  Subnet mask: _____

  (This is required to indicate the IP network for the personal computer.)

  Default gateway: _____

  (This is the address of the router.)

  DHCP server: _____

  (Your computer received address information from this computer.)

  DNS servers (you may have more than one): _____

  _____

  _____

  (This server will resolve host names to IP addresses.)

  Primary WINS server: _____

  (This computer will resolve computer names to IP addresses.)

  Secondary WINS server: _____

  Lease obtained: _____

  (You got your IP lease at this date and time.)

  Lease expires: _____

  (Your IP lease should be renewed before this date and time.)

Certification Objectives

Objectives for Microsoft Exam 70-215: Installing, Configuring, and Administering Microsoft Windows 2000 Server:

➤ Install, configure, and troubleshoot network protocols

➤ Install, configure, and troubleshoot network adapters and drivers

Review Questions

1. What is the best program to use to find the IP configuration on a Windows 2000 server?

  a. Device Manager

  b. ipconfig

  c. Windows 2000 Hardware Qualifier

  d. System Monitor

2. Joe calls on the phone. He is confused about the addresses that are displayed by the ipconfig command. He sees a number of addresses in dotted decimal. He needs to know which dotted decimal address is the logical address for the network adapter. What do you tell him?

a. physical address

b. IP address

c. subnet mask

d. default gateway

LAB 3.2 DETERMINE TCP/IP CONNECTIVITY

Objectives

The goal of this lab is to test connectivity to a remote host by systematically using the ping command. The ping is your first choice when troubleshooting. Ping is a tool that verifies IP-level connectivity. You can use ping to isolate system configuration problems and network hardware problems. After completing this lab, you will be able to:

➤ Verify that the TCP/IP stack functions

➤ Verify connectivity to the network adapter

➤ Verify connectivity to another host on the local segment

➤ Verify connectivity to a host on a remote segment

Materials Required

This lab will require the following:

➤ Access to a computer with Windows 2000 Professional or Server with the TCP/IP protocol installed

➤ Access to another network segment through a router

Activity Background

Table 3-1 presents a summary of the logic for each step in the ping test process. You will need this information for the connectivity tests in this lab.

Table 3-1   Systematic Ping Test

If you ping . . .	You will verify that the . . .
Loopback Address 127.0.0.1	TCP/IP stack is installed and configured correctly
IP address of the local computer	Computer was recognized by the network adapter
IP address of the default gateway	Computer can communicate with a local host on the local network
IP address of a remote host	Computer can communicate through a router to remote network

Estimated completion time: **30 minutes**

ACTIVITY

3

1. To test the TCP/IP stack, type **ping 127.0.0.1**, and then press **Enter**. If it tests successfully, you will see Reply from 127.0.0.1.... If it pings unsuccessfully, you will see an error message that indicates that the TCP/IP software is not operating correctly.

2. To test connectivity to the network adapter, type **ping *IP address***, where *IP address* is the IP address of the network adapter in Lab 3.1, Step 4, and then press **Enter**. If it tests successfully, you will see Reply from *IP address*.... If it tests unsuccessfully, you will see an error message that indicates that the network adapter is not operating correctly.

3. To test connectivity to a host on the local segment, type **ping *default gateway***, where *default gateway* is the default gateway of the network adapter in Lab 3.1, Step 4, and then press **Enter**. If it tests successfully, you will see Reply from *IP address*....

4. Choose the IP address of a remote host (DHCP server, DNS server, or primary WINS) of the network adapter in Lab 3.1. To test connectivity to the host on the remote segment, type **ping *IP address***, where *IP address* is the IP address of the remote host you chose, and then press **Enter**. If it tests successfully, you will see Reply from *IP address*....

5. Close the **command prompt** window.

Certification Objectives

Objectives for Microsoft Exam 70-215: Installing, Configuring, and Administering Microsoft Windows 2000 Server:

➤ Install, configure, and troubleshoot network protocols

➤ Install and configure network services for interoperability

Review Questions

1. Stephen wants to find out if he can reach a host with an IP address of 172.16.33.248. Which command line utility would you tell Stephen to use?
   a. Ping
   b. NBTStat
   c. FTP
   d. Tracert
   e. NSLookup

2. Joe installed a new card on his PC, which is part of a Windows 2000 network with multiple LAN segments. He is now installing the TCP/IP protocol. To finish his installation, what does Joe need to know?

a. IP address

b. subnet mask

c. gateway address

d. MAC address

3. You configured your Windows 2000 Server. What utilities will allow you to check that your configuration is correct?

a. Tracert

b. Stack

c. Ping

d. Ipconfig

e. Ipcheck

4. Antonio asks for your help in testing his Windows 2000 Server connection. He has pinged the remote host and received a negative response. What should Antonio do next?

a. He should ping the server IP address, ping the gateway address, and then ping the remote host.

b. He should ping the remote host until it answers with a positive response.

c. He should ping the local host, ping the server IP address, ping the gateway address, and then ping the remote host.

d. He should ping the server IP address, ping the remote host, and then ping the gateway address.

LAB 3.3 REVIEW IP ADDRESSING

Objectives

The goal of this lab is to review IP addressing concepts. As a network administrator, you must be prepared to use IP addressing for the personal computers in your network. After completing this lab, for a given IP address, you will be able to:

➤ Provide the class

➤ Provide the default subnet mask

➤ Determine the network

➤ Determine the host

➤ Determine the network using a custom subnet mask

➤ Interpret network number and host ranges when using custom subnetting

Materials Required

This lab will require the following:

➤ Access to *MCSE Guide to Windows 2000 Server* for each student

Activity Background

IP addresses are 32-bit addresses represented as dotted decimal numbers. For example, the Web server at the White House has an IP address of 198.137.240.92. To meet the address requirements of various size organizations, IP addresses are grouped into categories. Table 3-2 summarizes key information regarding IP addresses.

Table 3-2   IP Address Categories

Address Class	Address Range	Default Subnet Mask
A	001–126	255.0.0.0
B	128–191	255.255.0.0
C	192–223	255.255.255.0

The default subnet mask identifies the network and host components. For example, the IP address 172.16.23.78 with a default subnet mask of 255.255.0.0 splits into a network of 172.16.0.0 and a host of 0.0.23.78.

With a custom subnet mask, the administrator carves out more networks by borrowing from the host bits. For example, the IP network 172.31.0.0 with a custom subnet mask of 255.255.224.0 provides six networks. Table 3-3 summarizes the networks, host ranges, and local broadcasts for the example. Notice that the network addresses increment by 32.

Table 3-3   IP Network 172.31.0.0 Subnetted

Networks	Host Ranges	Local Broadcasts
172.31.32.0	172.31.32.1–172.31.63.254	172.31.63.255
172.31.64.0	172.31.64.1–172.31.95.254	172.31.95.255
172.31.96.0	172.31.96.1–172.31.127.254	172.31.127.255
172.31.128.0	172.31.128.1–172.31.159.254	172.31.159.255
172.31.160.0	172.31.160.1–172.31.191.254	172.31.191.255
172.31.192.0	172.31.192.1–172.31.223.254	172.31.223.255

Estimated completion time: **30 minutes**

ACTIVITY

1. Identify the network class for each of the networks in Table 3-4. A sample answer appears in the first row.

Table 3-4   IP Network Classes

Network	Network class
10.0.0.0	A
165.12.0.0	
203.24.32.0	
64.0.0.0	
198.45.89.0	

2. Provide the default subnet mask for each of the networks in Table 3-5. A sample answer appears in the first row.

Table 3-5   Default Subnet Mask

Network	Default Subnet Mask
10.0.0.0	255.0.0.0
65.12.0.0	
204.24.32.0	
170.123.0.0	

3. Provide the network and host for each of the IP addresses in Table 3-6. A sample answer appears in the first row.

Table 3-6   Network and Host

IP Address	Subnet Mask	Network	Host
10.10.0.5	255.0.0.0	10.0.0.0	0.10.0.5
165.234.89.244	255.255.0.0		
203.24.32.7	255.255.255.0		
64.89.56.9	255.255.255.0		
198.45.89.88	255.255.255.224		

Certification Objectives

Objectives for Microsoft Exam 70-215: Installing, Configuring, and Administering Microsoft Windows 2000 Server:

➤ Install, configure, and troubleshoot network protocols

➤ Install and configure network services for interoperability

3

Review Questions

1. Brian asks you what class of address is based on IP address 204.198.12.45. What do you tell him?

   a. A

   b. B

   c. C

   d. D

2. George has IP address 172.18.36.12 and subnet mask 255.255.0.0 for his host. What is the network address of his personal computer?

   a. 172.18.36.0

   b. 172.18.36.1

   c. 172.18.0.0

   d. 172.0.0.0

   e. none of the above

3. You are asked to resolve a problem with two computers. You use the ipconfig command and determine the IP addresses of the two computers. The IP address for Alice's computer is 172.31.35.12 and the subnet mask is 255.255.224.0. Alice is unable to communicate with Bob's computer on the same physical segment that has an IP address of 172.31.65.13 and a subnet mask of 255.255.224.0. What is required to correct the problem?

   a. She should change the IP address of Bob's computer to 172.31.35.12.

   b. She should change the IP address of Bob's computer to 172.31.65.12.

   c. She should change the IP address of Bob's computer to an IP address in the range of 172.31.32.1–172.31.63.254.

   d. She should change the IP address of Bob's computer to an IP address in the range of 172.31.32.1–172.31.47.254.

4. BigT needs to set up a TCP/IP network that consists of four personal computers running Windows 2000 Server, 200 personal computers running Windows 2000 Professional, and 50 personal computers running Windows 98.

   Required objective:

➤ Use a class B addressing scheme

Optional objectives:

➤ Configure at least 256 hosts on each subnet

➤ Set up at least six different subnets on the network

The proposed solution is to use a private B address of 172.16.0.0 and a subnet mask of 255.255.224.0. What does the proposed solution provide?

a. required result and both optional results

b. required result and one optional result

c. required result and no optional results

d. proposed solution does not provide required result

LAB 3.4 INSTALL AND REMOVE THE NetBEUI PROTOCOL (OPTIONAL LAB)

Objectives

The goal of this optional lab is to install and remove the NetBEUI network protocol. As a network administrator, you are required to install and remove network protocols such as NetBEUI, TCP/IP, or NWLink. After completing this lab, you will be able to:

➤ Install the NetBEUI protocol

➤ Uninstall the NetBEUI protocol

Materials Required

This lab will require the following:

➤ Access as an administrator to a computer with Windows 2000 Professional or Server with an existing network connection other than NetBEUI

Activity Background

The NetBEUI protocol supports small peer-to-peer networks. Recall that the NetBEUI protocol is non-routable and self-configuring.

Estimated completion time: **30 minutes**

ACTIVITY

1. As Administrator, log on to Windows 2000 Server or Professional. Right-click the **My Network Places** icon on the desktop, and then click **Properties**.

2. Right-click the **Local Area Connection** icon, and then click **Properties**.

3. Click the **Install** button, click **Protocol** in the Local Area Connection Properties dialog box, and then click the **Add** button.

4. Click **NetBEUI Protocol**, click **OK**, and then click **Close**.

5. Right-click the **Local Area Connection** icon, and then click **Properties**.

6. Click **NetBEUI Protocol** in the Local Area Connection Properties dialog box, and then observe the **Properties** button. Notice that the properties box is grayed out because the NetBEUI protocol is self-configuring.

7. Read the description for the NetBEUI protocol.

8. Locate and click **NetBEUI Protocol** in the Local Area Connection Properties dialog box, and then click the **Uninstall** button to uninstall the NetBEUI protocol.

9. Click the **Yes** button to confirm the uninstall of NetBEUI.

10. Click the **Yes** button to restart your computer.

Certification Objectives

Objectives for Microsoft Exam 70-215: Installing, Configuring, and Administering Microsoft Windows 2000 Server:

➤ Install, configure, and troubleshoot network protocols

Review Question

1. Lillie and Brian are discussing the properties of the NetBEUI network protocol. They ask you to summarize the discussion. What will you tell them about the protocol?
   a. It is routable.
   b. It is non-routable.
   c. It is self-configuring.
   d. It is used with peer-to-peer networks.
   e. It is used with server-based networks.

2. John asks you to provide the correct sequence of steps to display the properties of the TCP/IP protocol for a personal computer running Windows 2000 Server. Indicate the correct sequence of steps to display the Local Area Connection Properties dialog box.
   1. Click the Properties button.
   2. Click the TCP/IP Protocol.
   3. Click Properties.
   4. Right-click the Local Area Connection icon.
   5. Right-click the My Network Places icon.
      a. 4, 2, 1
      b. 4, 5, 3, 3, 2, 1
      c. 5, 4, 3, 2, 1
      d. 5, 3, 4, 3, 2, 1

LAB 3.5 INVESTIGATE NETWORK PROTOCOLS

Objectives

The goal of this lab is to investigate the Windows 2000 Server network protocol options (TCP/IP, NWLink, and NetBEUI). As a network administrator, you will evaluate the need for the various network protocol implementations for your servers. After completing this lab, you will be able to:

➤ Launch Windows 2000 Help

➤ Research the network protocols of Windows 2000 Server

Materials Required

This lab will require the following:

➤ Access to a computer with Microsoft Windows 2000 Server

➤ Access to *MCSE Guide to Windows 2000 Server* for each student

Estimated completion time: **30 minutes**

ACTIVITY

1. Click **Start**, and then click **Help**. If necessary, click the **Show** icon to display the tabs for Contents, Index, and Search.

2. Click the **Search** tab, type **NetBEUI defined** in the Type in the word(s) to search for text box, and then click **List Topics.**

3. Click **NetBEUI defined**, and then click **Display**.

4. Read the information regarding the NetBEUI protocol implementation for Windows 2000 Server.

5. Type **TCP/IP Overview** in the Type in the word(s) to search for text box, and then click **List Topics**.

6. Click **TCP/IP overview**, and then click **Display**.

7. Click the **TCP/IP background** link.

8. Read the information regarding the background for TCP/IP.

9. Click the **Back** button.

10. Click the **TCP/IP for Windows 2000** link.

11. Read the information about the TCP/IP implementation in Windows 2000 Server.

12. Type **IPX/SPX Defined** in the Type in the word(s) to search for text box, and then click **List Topics**.

13. Click **IPX/SPX defined**, and then click **Display**.

14. Read the information regarding the IPX/SPX (NWLink) implementation in Windows 2000 Server.

15. Close the **Help** window.

Certification Objectives

Objectives for Microsoft Exam 70-215: Installing, Configuring, and Administering Microsoft Windows 2000 Server:

➤ Install, configure, and troubleshoot network protocols

➤ Install and configure network services for interoperability

Review Questions

1. Joanne read about the exciting new features of the Internet. Which protocol does she need to install to make her computers Internet ready?
   a. TCP/IP
   b. NWLink (IPX/SPX)
   c. NetBEUI
   d. AppleTalk

2. Which of the following protocols are used with NetWare servers?
   a. IPX/SPX
   b. TCP/IP
   c. NetBEUI
   d. AppleTalk

3. Which Microsoft network protocol is compatible with IPX/SPX?
   a. NWLink
   b. IPX
   c. NetBEUI
   d. TCP/IP

4. You are interviewing for a networking job. The interviewer asks you to identify the Microsoft default network protocol. Being a Windows 2000 guru, you answer NetBEUI. What does the interviewer say?
   a. "You are correct and you get the job."
   b. "TCP/IP is the default protocol. Study harder."
   c. "IPX/SPX is the default protocol and you forgot about Novell."
   d. "AppleTalk is the default protocol. Let's discuss the new Apple computers."

CHAPTER FOUR

PLANNING THE ACTIVE DIRECTORY AND SECURITY

Labs included in this chapter

➤ Lab 4.1 Plan for the LoneStar Windows 2000 Network

➤ Lab 4.2 Install Active Directory (Optional)

➤ Lab 4.3 Create the LoneStar Organizational Units

➤ Lab 4.4 Create LoneStar Computer Names

Microsoft MCSE Exam #70-215 Objectives	
Objective	Lab
Perform an attended installation of Windows 2000	4.1
Install and configure network services for interoperability	4.2
Monitor, configure, troubleshoot, and control access to files, folders, and shared folders	4.2, 4.3, 4.4
Manage and optimize availability of system state data and user data	4.2, 4.3
Install, configure, and troubleshoot shared access	4.2, 4.3, 4.4

LAB 4.1 PLAN FOR THE LONESTAR WINDOWS 2000 NETWORK

Objectives

The goal of this lab is to finalize the network design for LoneStar. The Windows 2000 network for LoneStar will be implemented in successive lab activities. After completing this lab, you will be able to:

➤ Specify a domain name

➤ Specify the names for computers

➤ Specify the organizational units for computers

Materials Required

This lab will require the following:

➤ Access to *MCSE Guide to Windows 2000 Server* for each student

Activity Background

LoneStar markets imprinted shirts and caps. After years of successful operation, LoneStar expanded to three cities: Austin, Dallas, and Houston. Each city has numerous personal computers.

LoneStar now wants to deploy Windows 2000 Server and Professional in their three offices. LoneStar also wants to network their personal computers to share file and printer resources. In addition, LoneStar needs to communicate between the three cities.

You will prepare technical documentation for the owner/manager of LoneStar. You must specify a domain name, organizational units, and computer names. Figure 4-1 provides the first cut at a network diagram for LoneStar.

LoneStar

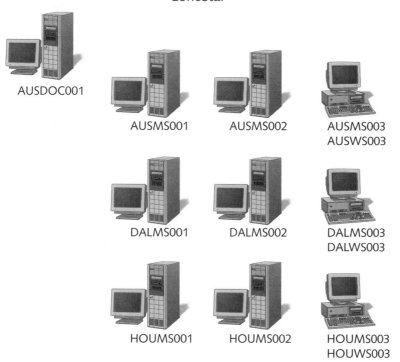

Figure 4-1   Working Version

This activity can be completed as a class activity. Your instructor may expand the design to include additional computers running Windows 2000 Server, and additional computers running Windows 2000 Professional. Also, your instructor may include additional organizational units

Estimated completion time: **30 minutes**

ACTIVITY

1. Specify the domain name for the Windows 2000 network. The name should be an Internet name, such as lonestar.com. _____

2. Specify the sites at which Windows 2000 member servers and the test Windows 2000 Professional personal computers will be installed.

_____

_____

_____

_____

3. Using the criteria provided below, provide computer names for the Windows 2000 member servers. Then, provide a computer name for the Windows 2000 Professional personal computer that you will test at each site.

For the computer names, use the following criteria:

- Computer names contain 8-15 characters (A-Z, 0-9).

- Computer names represent functions, not persons.

- Computer names follow uniform coding.

- Computer names are meaningful.

For example, a computer name that follows the criteria would be WACMS001. The computer resides in the city of Waco (WAC). The computer is a member server (MS) and it is the first member server (001).

Austin _____

_____

_____

_____

Dallas _____

Houston _____

LAB 4.2 INSTALL ACTIVE DIRECTORY (OPTIONAL)

Objectives

The goal of this lab is to install the Active Directory and the Domain Name System (DNS) for the LoneStar domain. After completing this lab, you will be able to:

➤ Utilize the Active Directory Wizard to install an active directory

➤ Utilize the Active Directory Wizard to install the Directory Name System (DNS)

Materials Required

This lab will require the following:

➤ Administrative access to a computer with Windows 2000 Member Server. The computer running Windows 2000 Member Server will be converted to function as a Windows 2000 Domain Controller.

Note

This lab can be completed as a class activity. Your instructor may expand the design to include additional computers running Windows 2000 Server, and additional computers running Windows 2000 Professional. Also, your instructor may include additional organizational units.

Estimated completion time: **60 minutes**

ACTIVITY

1. As administrator, log on to a computer running Windows 2000 Member Server.

2. Click **Start**, point to **Programs**, point to **Administrative Tools**, and then click **Configure Your Server**.

3. Click **Active Directory** in the left pane.

4. Scroll down in the right pane, and then click **Start the Active Directory wizard**.

5. Click **Next** in the Active Directory Installation Wizard.

6. Click **Domain controller for a new domain**. Click **Next**.

7. Click **Create a new domain tree**. Click **Next**.

8. Click **Create a new forest of domain trees**. Click **Next**.

9. Enter the domain name specified in Lab 4.1, Step 1 in the Full DNS name for new domain text box. (Remember that the name should be an Internet name, such as lonestar.com.) Click **Next**.

10. You will see a similar name presented in the Domain NetBIOs name text box. Leave the name as is, and then click **Next**.

11. Leave C:\WINNT\NTDS as the database location and C:\WINNT\NTDS as the log location (you could be using a different path to the location of the \WINNT folder). Click **Next**.

12. Leave the shared system volume as the default C:\WINNT\SYSVOL (the path will depend on the location of the \WINNT folder). Click **Next**. The wizard may warn that the SYSVOL must be on a partition formatted as NTFS version 5. If so, click **Next** and then click **OK**.

13. Click the **Yes, install and configure DNS on this computer (recommended)** option button, and then click **Next**.

14. You can use permissions compatible with pre-Windows 2000 servers, such as Windows NT Server 4.0, or you can use permissions compatible with Windows 2000 servers. Since we may want to use Windows 4.0 servers and workstations, click **Permissions compatible with pre-Windows 2000 servers**, and then click **Next**.

15. Type the Administrator password and confirm it for use in the Directory Services Restore Mode. Click **Next**.

16. Review the scroll box of choices, and then click **Next**.

17. Wait for the wizard to complete the Active Directory configuration. Observe the line near the bottom of the dialog box that indicates when each task is completed.

18. Click **Finish**.

19. **Close** any open applications. Click **Restart Now**.

Certification Objectives

Objectives for Microsoft Exam 70-215: Installing, Configuring, and Administering Microsoft Windows 2000 Server:

➤ Monitor, configure, troubleshoot, and control access to files, folders, and shared folders

➤ Manage and optimize availability of system state data and user data

➤ Install, configure, and troubleshoot shared access

Review Questions

1. The Windows 2000 Domain Controller is properly described by which of the following statements?

   a. It requires Windows 2000 Professional.

   b. It can be promoted from a member server.

   c. It can be demoted to a member server.

   d. It maintains the Active Directory.

   e. It is selected as a domain controller during installation.

2. Josh inquires about the differences between Windows NT 4.0 domains and Windows 2000 domains. Which items would you include in your discussion with Josh?

   a. Windows NT 4.0 domains have primary/backup domain controllers.

   b. Windows 2000 domains have peer domain controllers.

   c. Windows NT 4.0 domains require Active Directory.

   d. Windows 2000 domains require Active Directory.

   e. Windows NT 4.0 domains are more scalable.

3. BigB needs to set up a Windows 2000 network that consists of six sites within the United States (Los Angeles, Boston, St. Louis, Denver, Knoxville, and Dallas) and two sites in Europe (Berlin and London). Financial groups are located in Chicago and Berlin.

   Required objective:

   ■ Implement a Windows 2000 network with Active Directory

   Optional objectives:

   ■ Minimize traffic on the Wide Area Network (WAN) link between the United States and Europe

   ■ Provide administrative control for the financial groups in Chicago and Berlin

The proposed solution is to implement a single domain with a Windows 2000 domain controller. An organizational unit is established for the financial group in Chicago and Berlin. Other organizational groups coincide with geographical locations. What does the proposed solution provide?

a. required result and both optional results

b. required result and one optional result

c. required result and no optional results

d. solution does not meet required result

4

LAB 4.3 CREATE THE LONESTAR ORGANIZATIONAL UNITS

Objectives

The goal of this lab is to create the organizational units for LoneStar. After completing this lab, you will be able to:

➤ Start the Active Directory Users and Computers

➤ Create Organizational Unit containers

Materials Required

This lab will require the following:

➤ Administrative access to a computer with Windows 2000 Domain Controller with the Active Directory for LoneStar

Estimated completion time: 30 minutes

ACTIVITY

1. As Administrator, log on to the Windows 2000 Domain Controller with the Active Directory for LoneStar.

2. Click **Start**, point to **Programs**, point to **Administrative Tools**, and then click **Active Directory Users and Computers**.

3. Click the plus sign next to **lonestar.com** in the left pane. (Your domain name might differ.) Figure 4-2 shows lonestar.com expanded.

4. Select the domain name, click the **Action** button, point to **New**, and then click **Organizational Unit**. Type **Austin**, and then click **OK**. Figure 4-3 shows the Organizational Unit dialog box.

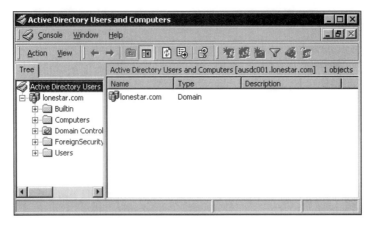

Figure 4-2   LoneStar.com Expanded

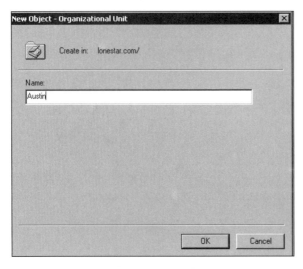

Figure 4-3   Enter Organizational Unit

     5. Repeat Step 4 for Dallas and Houston. Figure 4-4 shows all the newly added cities.

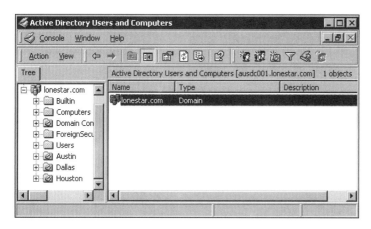

Figure 4-4   Cities Added to Active Directory

    6. Leave the Active Directory Users and Computers pane open for the next lab
activity.

Certification Objectives

Objectives for Microsoft Exam 70-215: Installing, Configuring, and Administering Microsoft
Windows 2000 Server:

➤ Monitor, configure, troubleshoot, and control access to files, folders, and shared
folders

➤ Manage and optimize availability of system state data and user data

➤ Install, configure, and troubleshoot shared access

Review Questions

    1. Brian wants to explain organizational units to Rose. Which of the following
statements about organizational units is true?

      a. They are container objects.

      b. They cannot contain other organizational units.

      c. They contain users and groups.

      d. They contain other organizational units.

      e. They contain resources.

    2. Brian is explaining container objects to Rose. Which of the following statements
will Brian make to Rose?

      a. Container objects have attributes.

      b. They are part of the Active Directory namespace.

      c. They do not usually represent something concrete.

      d. The organizational unit is an example of a container object.

      e. They can contain other containers.

3. In what order do you execute the following steps to add an organizational unit with the Active Directory Users and Computers?

1. Select a container (domain or OU).
2. Click Organizational Unit.
3. Select Action.
4. Point to New.
5. Type name.
6. Click OK.

   a. 3, 1, 4, 2, 5, 6
   b. 1, 3, 4, 2, 5, 6
   c. 1, 3, 2, 4, 5, 6
   d. 3, 1, 2, 4, 5, 6

4. Organizational units are structures that you use to organize objects. Which items can be added to organizational units?

   a. groups
   b. users
   c. domains
   d. organizational units
   e. computers

LAB 4.4 CREATE LONESTAR COMPUTER NAMES

Objectives

The goal of this lab is to add computer names to the proper organizational units. After completing this lab, you will be able to:

➤ Locate an organizational unit

➤ Add a computer to an organizational unit

Materials Required

This lab will require the following:

➤ Access to a computer with Windows 2000 Domain Controller with the Active Directory for LoneStar

➤ Completion of Lab 4.3

Estimated completion time: **30 minutes**

ACTIVITY

1. Click **Austin** in the Active Directory Computer Users pane.

2. Click **Action**, point to **New**, click **Computer**, and then type **ausms001**. Leave the Computer Name as AUSMS001. Click **OK**. Your screen should resemble Figure 4-5.

4

Figure 4-5   New Object Computer Dialog Box

3. Repeat Step 2 for the remaining member server, ausms002.

4. Click **Action**, point to **New**, and then click **Computer**. Type **ausws003**. Leave the Computer Name as AUSWS003. Click **Allow pre-Windows 2000 computers to use this account**. (Pre-Windows 2000 computers and Windows NT 4.0 workstations require this option.) Click **OK**.

5. Repeat Steps 1 through 4 for the computers in the remaining organizational units. Your screen should resemble Figure 4-6.

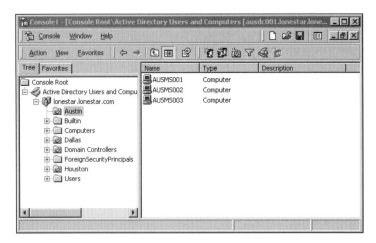

Figure 4-6   Houston Added to Active Directory

Certification Objectives

Objectives for Microsoft Exam 70-215: Installing, Configuring, and Administering Microsoft Windows 2000 Server:

➤ Monitor, configure, troubleshoot, and control access to files, folders, and shared folders

➤ Manage and optimize availability of system state data and user data

➤ Install, configure, and troubleshoot shared access

Review Questions

1. In what order do you execute the following steps to add a computer to an organizational unit with Active Directory Users and Computers?

   1. Type the computer name.
   2. Select container in the left pane.
   3. Select Action.
   4. Click Computer.
   5. Point to New.
   6. Click OK.

      a. 3, 2, 5, 4, 1, 6
      b. 2, 3, 4, 5, 1, 6
      c. 2, 3, 5, 4, 1, 6
      d. 3, 2, 4, 5, 1, 6

2. Brian and Lillie are entering computer names at the New Object - Computer dialog box. Brian typed dallas01 for the computer name. Lillie notices that DALLAS01 appears in the Computer Name (pre–Windows 2000) text box. Lillie asks Brian the reason for the two names. How does Brian respond? (Choose all correct answers.)

   a. The Domain Name System (DNS) requires a host name.

   b. The Domain Name System (DNS) requires a NetBIOS name.

   c. The pre–Windows 2000 Computer Name is used with peer-to-peer networks.

   d. Windows 2000 creates Fully Qualified Domain Names (FQDN) by appending the domain name to the computer name.

   e. All of the above are true.

4

CHAPTER FIVE

SERVER INSTALLATION

Labs included in this chapter

➤ Lab 5.1 View Winnt32 Switches

➤ Lab 5.2 Install the SetupMgr

➤ Lab 5.3 Create an Unattended Answer File

➤ Lab 5.4 Create the Windows 2000 Server Installation Disks

➤ Lab 5.5 Install Windows 2000 Server with Installation Disks (Optional Lab)

➤ Lab 5.6 Set a Static IP Address

Microsoft MCSE Exam #70-215 Objectives	
Objective	Lab
Perform an attended installation of Windows 2000	5.1, 5.4, 5.5
Perform an unattended installation of Windows 2000 Server	5.1, 5.2, 5.3
Troubleshoot failed installations	5.1, 5.2, 5.3, 5.4, 5.5
Install, configure, and troubleshoot network protocols	5.6

Lab 5.1 View Winnt32 Switches

Objectives

The goal of this lab is to view the option switches that can be used with the Winnt32 installation program. As a network administrator, you will use the option switches to control the installation of Windows 2000 Server. After completing this lab, you will be able to:

➤ Run a Windows operating system command program

➤ View the option switches for the Winnt32 command

➤ Summarize the critical Windows 2000 Server installation switches

Materials Required

This lab will require the following:

➤ Access to a computer with a Microsoft Windows operating system (Windows 95 or 98, Windows NT 4.0, or Windows 2000)

➤ A Windows 2000 Server CD-ROM

Estimated completion time: **30 minutes**

Activity

1. If you are using a personal computer with Windows 95 or 98, do the following, and then go to Step 4 where you will summarize your research:
   a. Insert the Windows 2000 Server CD-ROM into the CD-ROM drive.
   b. Click **No** if the upgrade message appears.
   c. Click **Exit** if the Microsoft Windows 2000 CD dialog box appears.
   d. Click **Start**. Click **Programs**, and then click **MS-DOS Prompt**.
   e. Type **CD-ROM drive:\i386\winnt32 /?**, where *CD-ROM drive* is the drive letter of your CD-ROM, and then press **Enter**.
   f. Review the switches.

2. If you are using a personal computer with Windows NT 4.0, do the following, and then go to Step 4 where you will summarize your research:
   a. Insert the Windows 2000 Server CD-ROM, into the CD-ROM drive.
   b. Click **No** if the upgrade message appears.
   c. Click **Exit** if the Microsoft Windows 2000 CD dialog box appears.
   d. Click the **Start** button on the taskbar.
   e. Point to **Programs**, and then click **Command Prompt.**
   f. Type **CD-ROM drive:\i386\winnt32 /?**, where *CD-ROM drive* is the drive letter of your CD-ROM, and then press **Enter**.
   g. Review the switches.

3. If you are using a personal computer with Windows 2000, do the following, and then go to Step 4 where you will summarize your research:

   a. Insert the Windows 2000 Server CD-ROM into the CD-ROM drive.

   b. Click **Exit** if the Microsoft Windows 2000 CD dialog box appears.

   c. Click **Start**, point to **Programs**, point to **Accessories**, and then click **Command Prompt**.

   d. Type **CD-ROM drive:\i386\winnt32 /?**, where *CD-ROM drive* is the drive letter of your CD-ROM, and then press **Enter**.

   e. Review the switches.

4. To summarize the critical Windows 2000 installation switches, complete Table 5-1.

5. Close the Command Prompt window.

Table 5-1   Typical Winnt32 Switches

Switch	Record Purpose of Switch
/?	
/cmd:command	
/comdcons	
/copydir:folder	
/copysource:folder	
/makelocalsource	
/S:\\server\share\folder	
/tempdrive:drive	
/unattend:script	
/Udf:id,udffile	

Certification Objectives

Objectives for Microsoft Exam 70-215: Installing, Configuring, and Administering Microsoft Windows 2000 Server:

➤ Perform an attended installation of Windows 2000 Server

➤ Perform an unattended installation of Windows 2000 Server

➤ Troubleshoot failed installations

Review Questions

1. Your personal computer is several years old and has Microsoft Windows NT 4.0 installed. You must run the Winnt32 program to see if the computer is ready to run Windows 2000 Server. Which Winnt32 switch will create a compatibility report?

   a. /hcl

   b. /debug

   c. /checkupgradeonly

   d. /check

2. Victoria wants to copy the Windows 2000 CD-ROM source files to a server. Victoria points out that this will permit changes to a server without reinserting the Windows 2000 CD-ROM. Which switch will accomplish this task?

   a. /m:source

   b. /copydir:source

   c. /copysource/source

   d. /makelocalsource

LAB 5.2 INSTALL THE SETUPMGR

Objectives

The goal of this lab is to install the SetupMgr. You will use the SetupMgr to create the text file for unattended installations of Windows 2000 Server. The SetupMgr is required to complete Lab 5.3. After completing this lab, you will be able to:

➤ Use Windows Explorer to create a folder

➤ Copy files from one folder to another folder

➤ Install the SetupMgr tool

Materials Required

This lab will require the following:

➤ Access to a computer with Windows 2000 Server

➤ The Windows 2000 Server CD-ROM

Estimated completion time: **30 minutes**

ACTIVITY

1. Insert the Windows 2000 Server CD-ROM into the CD-ROM drive.

2. Select **Exit** if the Microsoft Windows 2000 CD dialog box appears.

3. Click **Start**. Point to **Programs**, point to **Accessories**, and then click **Windows Explorer**.

4. Click **My Computer** in the left pane. Double-click **Local Disk (C:)**.

5. Right-click anywhere in the white space in the right pane, point to **New**, click **Folder**, and then type **SetupMgr**.

6. In Windows Explorer, click **My Computer**, right-click **CD-ROM**, and then click **Open**.

7. Double-click the **Support** folder, and then double-click the **Tools** folder.

8. Double-click **Deploy**.

9. Copy Setupmgx.exe and SetupMgr.dll to the folder that you created in Step 5.

10. Close Windows Explorer.

Certification Objectives

Objectives for Microsoft Exam 70-215: Installing, Configuring, and Administering Microsoft Windows 2000 Server:

➤ Perform an unattended installation of Windows 2000 Server

➤ Troubleshoot failed installations

Review Questions

1. Jill tries to remember the steps to create a folder using Windows Explorer. She is not sure of the exact sequence of steps. Can you help her by indicating the correct sequence of steps?

   1. Point to New.
   2. Right-click in the white space in the right pane.
   3. Click Folder.
   4. Type the new folder name.
   a. 1, 2, 3, 4
   b. 3, 4, 1, 2
   c. 2, 1, 3, 4
   d. 3, 4, 2, 1

LAB 5.3 CREATE AN UNATTENDED ANSWER FILE

Objective

The goal of this lab is to create an unattended answer file with SetupMgr.

When you must deploy many personal computers on a job, the SetupMgr can create answer files to automate the installation of Windows 2000 Server or Windows 2000 Professional personal computers that meet your group's specifications. Since you will not need to interact with each computer during the installation, the use of unattended files will speed up the installations. After completing this lab, you will be able to:

➤ Create an unattended answer file for a Windows 2000 Server installation

Materials Required

This lab will require the following:

➤ Access to a computer running Windows 2000 Server

➤ The Windows 2000 Server CD-ROM

➤ The completion of Lab 5.2

➤ A computer name for the personal computer

Estimated completion time: **30 minutes**

ACTIVITY

1. Click **Start**, click **Run**, click **Browse**, and then locate and click **SetupMgr** in the folder created in Lab 5.2, Step 5. Click the **Open** button, and then click **OK**.

2. After reading the Setup Wizard screen, click **Next**.

3. Click the **Create a new answer file** option button, and then click **Next**.

4. Select **Windows 2000 Unattended Installation**, and then click **Next**.

5. Click the **Windows 2000 Server** option button, and then click **Next**.

6. Click on each option for Select the level of user interaction during Windows Setup, and then read each description. As you read the information, complete Table 5-2.

Table 5-2   Level of User Interaction

User Interaction Option	Description
Provide defaults	
Fully automated	
Hide pages	
Read only	
GUI attended	

7. Select the **Fully automated** option button, as shown in Figure 5-1, and then click **Next**.

8. Click **I accept the terms of the License Agreement**, and then click **Next**.

9. Type your name and organization name, and then click **Next**.

10. Click the **Per seat** option button, and then click **Next**.

11. Type the computer name supplied by your instructor, as shown in Figure 5-2, click **Add**, and then click **Next**.

Figure 5-1   Selecting the Fully automated option button

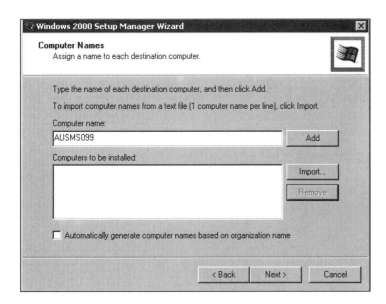

Figure 5-2   Specifying the computer name

12. Provide the password for the administrator account, and then click **Next**.

13. When the **Display Settings** appear, click **Next** to accept the defaults.

14. Retain the **Typical settings**, and then click **Next**.

15. Click **Windows Server domain** and then in the Windows Server domain text box, as shown in Figure 5-3, type **LoneStar**. Select the **Create a computer account in the domain** check box, type **administrator** for the user name, type an administrator password, confirm it, and then click **Next**.

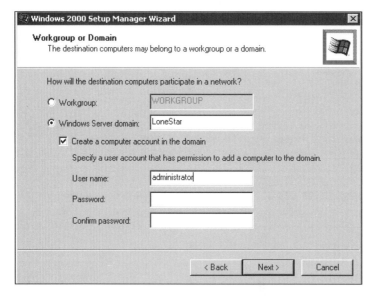

Figure 5-3   Selecting the domain and creating the computer account

16. Set the **time zone**, and then click **Next**.

17. Click **No, do not edit the additional settings**, and then click **Next**.

18. Click **No, the answer file will be used to install from CD**.

19. Review the answer file location, and then click **Next**.

If files have been left behind by another student who has used this wizard, you might see a message box after clicking Next. If so, click Yes.

20. Click **Finish**.

Certification Objectives

Objectives for Microsoft Exam 70-215: Installing, Configuring, and Administering Microsoft Windows 2000 Server:

➤ Perform an unattended installation of Windows 2000 Server

➤ Troubleshoot failed installations

Review Questions

1. Sally asks you if there is a tool in Windows 2000 Server that will assist in the installation of Windows 2000 Professional on multiple desktops. You recall that Windows 2000 Server has the SetupMgr. Sally asks you for additional information. Which of the following will you share with her?

   a. It creates an answer file to provide input during installation.

   b. It copies Windows 2000 Professional to a distribution folder.

   c. It installs Windows 2000 Professional to a computer from a server on the network.

   d. It starts without intervention from a technician.

2. You and Sally continue your discussion of unattended installation and the SetupMgr. She asks you about possible user interaction levels. Which of the following are available interaction levels?

   a. GUI attended

   b. Read only

   c. Fully automated

   d. Provide defaults

3. Brian is upgrading multiple existing Windows NT 4.0 servers to Windows 2000 servers. Prior to starting the upgrade, he created a list of goals for the upgrade:

   Goal A: Install the servers over the network from the mainserver.

   Goal B: Use the shared folder w2ksrv for the distribution code.

   Goal C: Use the file server.txt created by the SetupMgr tool.

   Goal D: Use the file server.udf to specify the computer names for the new servers.

   Brian typed the following line to start the installation of computer BUSRV001:
   \\mainserver\w2ksrv\winnt32.exe /s:\\mainserver\w2ksrv\ /unattend:server.txt /udf:BUSRV001,server.udf

   Which goals will Brian achieve?

   a. Goal A

   b. Goal B

   c. Goal C

   d. Goal D

   e. No goals will be achieved.

LAB 5.4 CREATE THE WINDOWS 2000 SERVER INSTALLATION DISKS

Objectives

The goal of this lab is to create the Windows 2000 Server installation disks.

When working with older computers, you may need to install Windows 2000 Server from the installation disks because the computer will not start from the Windows 2000 Server CD-ROM. In addition, you will need the installation disks to install the drivers for SCSI or RAID adapters. After completing this lab, you will be able to:

➤ Prepare the four Windows 2000 Server installation disks

Materials Required

This lab will require the following:

➤ Access to a computer with Windows 2000 Server

➤ The Windows 2000 Server CD-ROM

➤ Four blank, formatted, high-density disks per student

Estimated completion time: **60 minutes**

ACTIVITY

The process that creates the setup disks will overwrite any existing files on the disks. You must verify that the disks do not contain critical files.

Check the disks to ensure that the tab on the side of each one is not set to "write-protect." This will eliminate an error message about the media being write-protected.

1. Insert the Windows 2000 Server CD-ROM into the CD-ROM drive.

Hold down the Shift key to avoid the Windows 2000 CD-ROM Autoplay.

2. Click **Exit** if the Microsoft Windows 2000 CD dialog box appears.

3. Click **Start**, and then click **Run**.

4. Type **CD-ROM drive:\bootdisk\makebt32**, where *CD-ROM drive* is the drive letter of your CD-ROM, and then click **OK**.

5. Insert a disk into the disk drive. Press the **a** key to indicate the drive letter.

6. Press **Enter** to start the process.

7. Once the copy is complete, remove the first disk, label the disk, and then insert the second disk. Press **Enter** to copy to this disk.

8. Repeat Step 7 for the remaining disks.

Certification Objectives

Objectives for Microsoft Exam 70-215: Installing, Configuring, and Administering Microsoft Windows 2000 Server:

➤ Perform an attended installation of Windows 2000 Server

➤ Troubleshoot failed installations

Review Questions

1. Brian and Lillie are unsure which program they should run to create the four Windows 2000 Server installation disks. They ask you for help. What will you tell them?

   a. D:\i386\winnt /ox

   b. D:\makeboot\makedisk.exe

   c. D:\makeboot\makebt32.exe

   d. You must download the disk images from the Microsoft Web site.

2. You have four disks. You are unsure of their contents. You proceed with the creation of the first of four Windows 2000 Server installation disks. What are the possible outcomes of your action?

   a. The disk contains files, and you must format the disk.

   b. The disk contains files, and you receive an error message.

   c. The disk contains files, and the files are over-written.

   d. The disk is write-protected, and you receive a message that the media is write-protected.

LAB 5.5 INSTALL WINDOWS 2000 SERVER WITH INSTALLATION DISKS (OPTIONAL LAB)

Objectives

The goal of this optional lab is to practice installing Windows 2000 Server with the disks created in Lab 5.4. You will find these disks useful when you install a third-party driver for a SCSI controller or a hardware RAID controller. After completing this lab, you will be able to:

➤ Start the installation of Windows 2000 Server from the installation disks

➤ Install Windows 2000 Server

This lab can be completed as an instructor-led class activity.

Materials Required

This lab will require the following:

➤ Access to a computer on which you can install Windows 2000 Server. This computer should have no operating system installed.

➤ The Windows 2000 Server CD-ROM

➤ The four disks created in Lab 5.4

➤ Additional configuration information from your instructor

Estimated completion time: **120 minutes**

Activity

1. With your computer turned off, insert Disk #1 into the A: drive of your computer.

2. Turn on your computer.

If you install through a third-party SCSI or RAID adapter, you press F6 when the blue screen first appears.

3. When requested, remove Disk #1, insert Disk #2, and then press **Enter**.

4. Repeat Step 3 for Disk #3 and Disk #4, noting that the disk numbers in the instructions will change accordingly.

If you install an evaluation version of Windows 2000, you will receive a Setup Notification. Read the information message, and then press Enter.

5. When the Setup screen appears, as shown in Figure 5-4, review the three options, and then press **Enter**.

6. When requested, insert the Windows 2000 Server CD, and then press **Enter**.

7. Read the Licensing Agreement, press the **Page Down** key to scroll, and then press **F8**.

When performing subsequent Windows 2000 Server installations, you can press F8 to skip the license text.

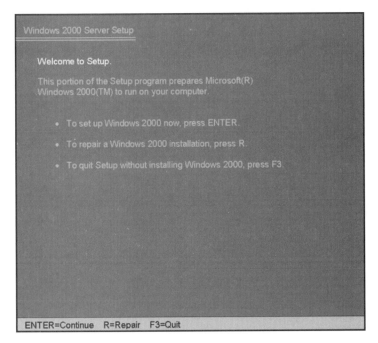

Figure 5-4   Windows 2000 Server setup

8. If a previous copy of Windows 2000 is detected, you will be given the option to repair or install a fresh copy. Press **Esc** to install a fresh copy.

9. Review the existing partitions and unpartitioned space on your computer, as shown in Figure 5-5.

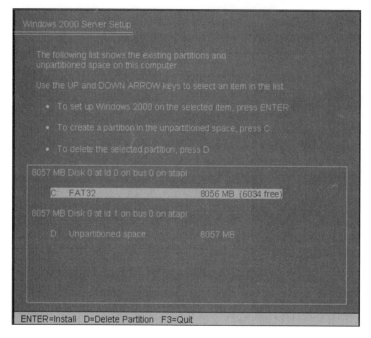

Figure 5-5 Selecting a location to install Windows 2000

10. Press the **UP ARROW** key or **DOWN ARROW** key to select a partition or unpartitioned space.

 To delete a partition, press D. To create a partition, select an unpartitioned space, and then press C. You will be asked to specify the amount of disk space. Recall that the default for Windows 2000 Server is 850 MB. A partition of 1 or 2 GB is adequate. If you choose to create a new partition, you will be prompted to format the partition using either NTFS or FAT.

11. When the partition has been selected, press **Enter** to start the install.

 If you attempt to install Windows 2000 on a partition that contains a previous version of Windows, you will receive the message "Installing Windows 2000 on this partition might cause the other operating system to function improperly." To select another partition, press Esc.

12. Select **Format the partition using the NTFS file system**, and then press **Enter**.

13. Wait while Setup checks your hard disk for errors and copies the appropriate files onto your hard disk.

14. When requested, remove the disk. The computer restarts and launches the Windows 2000 Setup Wizard.

15. Wait while the Setup Wizard detects and configures devices installed on your computer.

16. When the Regional Settings title appears, review the settings, and then click **Next**.

17. When the Personalize Your Software title appears, type the name of the person under which the computer will be registered. Press **Tab**, type the name of your organization, and then click **Next**.

18. When the Your Product Key title appears, type the 25-character **product key**. Click **Next**.

If you receive the message "The CD key you entered is not valid," click OK, and then type the correct product key.

5

19. When the Licensing Modes title appears, choose your licensing mode. Recall that per server is used for a single server installation and must enter the number of licenses. Click **Next**.

20. When the Computer Name and Administrator Password title appear, type the computer name provided by your instructor. Press **Tab**.

21. Type the password for the local administrator account. Press **Tab**. Retype the administrator password. Click **Next**.

If you receive the message "The passwords you entered do not match. Please enter the desired password again," press Enter, and then reenter the passwords.

22. When the Windows 2000 Components title appears, click **Next** to install the typical components.

23. Review the date, time, and time zone settings, change them as needed, and then click **Next**.

24. When the Network Settings title appears, review the options, select **Typical settings**, and then click **Next**.

25. When the Workgroup or Computer Domain title appears, select **Yes, Make the computer a member of following domain**, and then type **lonestar.com**. Click **Next**, type **administrator**, press **Tab**, then type the administrator password for the LoneStar domain, and then click **OK**.

26. When the Installing Components title appears, wait for the computer to install the remaining components.

27. When the Performing Final Tasks title appears, wait for the computer to perform the final tasks.

28. When the Completing the Windows 2000 Setup Wizard title appears, click **Finish**, and then remove the CD-ROM. In addition, take a moment to smile!

29. When the computer restarts, log on with the administrator account and password.

30. Clear the Show the screen at startup check box, and then close the window.

Certification Objectives

Objectives for Microsoft Exam 70-215: Installing, Configuring, and Administering Microsoft Windows 2000 Server:

➤ Perform an attended installation of Windows 2000 Server

➤ Troubleshoot failed installations

Review Questions

1. Rose asks for your help. She needs to know the alternate ways to install Windows 2000 Server. What will you tell Rose?
   a. Start from the first Windows 2000 Server installation disk.
   b. Start from the Windows 2000 Server CD-ROM.
   c. Install across the network.
   d. Launch Winnt32 from an existing Windows NT 4.0 installation.

2. You are installing Windows 2000 Server. Setup inspected the hardware configuration and loaded the drivers and other necessary files. At this point in the process, what are your options?
   a. Set up Windows 2000 Server.
   b Copy the files for a later installation.
   c. Repair an existing Windows 2000 installation.
   d. Quit Setup.

3. You are installing Windows 2000 Server. Setup inspected and located the existing partitions and unpartitioned space. At this point in the process, what are your options?
   a Convert from FAT32 to NTFS.
   b. Set up Windows 2000 on the highlighted partition.
   c. Delete the highlighted partition.
   d. Create a partition in the highlighted unpartitioned area.
   e. Quit Setup.

LAB 5.6 SET A STATIC IP ADDRESS

Objectives

The goal of this lab is to provide the static IP address for a Windows 2000 server. This address ensures consistent access to resources on Windows 2000 servers. In most organizations, static addresses are set aside for servers. After completing this lab, you will be able to:

> ➤ Enter a static IP address for a server

> ➤ Enter a subnet mask for a server

> ➤ Enter the static IP address for a Domain Name System (DNS) server

Materials Required

This lab will require the following:

> ➤ Access to a computer with Windows 2000 Server installed

> ➤ An IP address for the computer, and the IP address of the DNS server, which your instructor will provide. (Your instructor may furnish the subnet mask and the address of the default gateway.)

Estimated completion time: **30 minutes**

ACTIVITY

1. Right-click **My Network Places**, and then click **Properties**.

2. Right-click **Local Area Connections**, and then click **Properties**.

3. Click **Internet Protocol (TCP/IP)**. (Leave the the preceding check box as is.) Click **Properties**.

4. Click the **Help** button in the upper-right corner of your screen. Click the **IP address** text box. Read the Help text. Click to remove the Help text.

5. Click the **Use the following IP address** option button, and then type the IP address provided by your instructor.

Press the period key to advance to the next octet in the IP address.

6. Click the **Help** button, and then click the **Subnet mask** text box. Read the Help text. Click to remove the Help text.

7. Click the **Subnet mask** number. (The default subnet mask will be supplied. Or, you can type the subnet mask supplied by your instructor.)

8. Click **Use the following DNS server addresses**.

9. Click the **Help** button, and then click the **Preferred DNS server** text box. Read the Help text. Click to remove the Help text.

10. Type the **DNS address** provided by your instructor.

11. Click **OK**.

12. Click **OK**.

Certification Objectives

Objectives for Microsoft Exam 70-215:Installing, Configuring, and Administering Microsoft Windows 2000 Server:

➤ Install, configure, and troubleshoot network protocols

Review Questions

1. Indicate which of the following addresses are valid. Base your answer on information that you can obtain from Windows 2000 Help.

   a. 132.168.258.6

   b. 132,168,245,1

   c. 132.168..45

   d. 132.168.45.3

   e. 196.88.95.88

2. Joe asks you about the subnet mask field located in the Internet Protocol (TCP/IP) Properties dialog box. Which of the following will you share with Joe?

   a. It is obtained from a network administrator.

   b. With the IP address, it identifies the network for your computer.

   c. You type it as a 32-bit dotted-decimal number.

   d. It may be omitted from the configuration.

3. The Internet Protocol (TCP/IP) Properties dialog box contains the Preferred DNS server text box. Which of the following statements about the Preferred DNS server is true?

   a. It resolves name queries to IP addresses.

   b. It resolves name queries to MAC addresses.

   c. It resolves name queries to server names.

   d. It resolves name queries to memory addresses.

CHAPTER SIX

SERVER CONFIGURATION

Labs included in this chapter

➤ Lab 6.1 Change Folder Options

➤ Lab 6.2 Schedule a Task

➤ Lab 6.3 Set System Performance Options

➤ Lab 6.4 Review Resources with Device Manager

➤ Lab 6.5 Use Configure Your Server Wizard

Microsoft MCSE Exam #70-215 Objectives	
Objective	Lab
Perform an attended installation of Windows 2000	6.5
Install and configure network services for interoperability	6.5
Monitor, configure, troubleshoot, and control access to printers	6.5
Monitor, configure, troubleshoot, and control access to files, folders, and shared folders	6.5
Monitor, configure, control, and troubleshoot access to Web sites	6.5
Configure hardware devices	6.4
Configure driver signing options	6.4
Update device drivers	6.4
Troubleshoot problems with hardware	6.4
Monitor and optimize usage of system resources	6.3
Manage and optimize availability of system state data and user data	6.1, 6.2, 6.3
Recover systems and user data	6.2
Install and configure network services	6.5
Install, configure, and troubleshoot network adapters and drivers	6.4

LAB 6.1 CHANGE FOLDER OPTIONS

Objectives

The goal of this lab is to view and change the Folder Options. You can customize the folders that are displayed within Windows Explorer. This customization can greatly enhance your ability to locate and manipulate files that are required for day-to-day maintenance of your servers. Recall that Windows 2000 doesn't, by default, show you all the files and file extensions. After completing this lab, you will be able to:

➤ Run a Control Panel applet

➤ View the Folder Options

➤ Customize the Folder Options

Materials Required

This lab will require the following:

➤ Access as an administrator to a computer with Windows 2000 Server

Estimated completion time: **30 minutes**

ACTIVITY

1. You should be logged on to your computer as an administrator. Click **Start**, point to **Settings**, click **Control Panel**, and then double-click **Folder Options**.

2. Click the **General** tab. Click the **Help** button in the upper-right corner of the dialog box, and then click within the **Active Desktop** group. In order to become familiar with the various Folder Options, record your observations in Table 6-1.

3. Repeat Step 2 for the remaining three boxes on the General tab.

4. Leave the Folder Options dialog box open.

5. Click **Start**, point to **Programs**, point to **Accessories**, and then click **Windows Explorer**. Select the root folder for the C drive. (Note that your local disk may be under a different drive letter.)

Resize the Windows Explorer window to permit viewing of the Folder Options and Windows Explorer windows.

6. Return to the **Folder Options** dialog box, and then click the **View** tab. Your screen should resemble Figure 6-1.

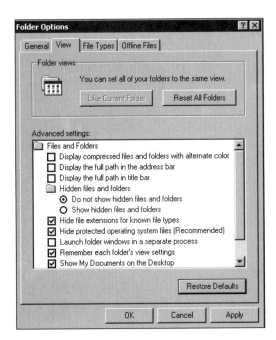

Figure 6-1   Folder Options view

7. Click **Display the full path in the address bar** check box to select it, click the **Display the full path in title bar** check box to select it, and then click **Apply**. Observe that the full paths appear in the address bar and window title bar.

8. Click the **Show hidden files and folders** option button to select it, and then click the **Hide file extensions for known file types** check box to deselect it. Click **Apply**. Notice that the hidden files appear, and the file extensions appear in the root folder displayed with Explorer.

 You can easily find files by selecting the Show hidden files and folders option button and deselecting the Hide file extensions for known file types check box.

9. Click **Restore Defaults** to return settings to the defaults, and then click **Apply**.

10. Click the **File Types** tab. Your screen will resemble Figure 6-2.

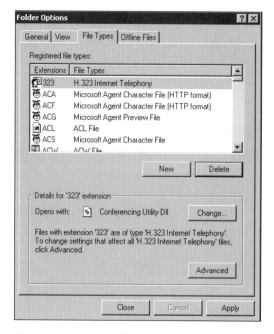

Figure 6-2   Folder file types

11. Click the **Help** button in the upper-right corner of the dialog box, and then click within the **Registered file types** list box. To become familiar with the various Folder Options, record your observations in Table 6-1.

12. **Close** all windows. Remain logged on as the administrator for the next lab.

Table 6-1   Folder Options

Option	Description
Active Desktop	
Web view	
Browse folders	
Check items as follows	
Registered file types	

Certification Objectives

Objectives for Microsoft Exam 70-215: Installing, Configuring, and Administering Microsoft Windows 2000 Server:

➤ Manage and optimize availability of system and user data

Review Questions

1. George noticed that when he works with multiple folders, his desktop becomes cluttered. Which of the following steps should George execute in what order to clear this clutter? Note that you might not need all the steps.

   1. Open Control Panel.
   2. Click the General tab.
   3. Double-click Folder Options.
   4. Click Open each folder in the same window.
   5. Click Apply.
   6. Click OK.

   a. 2, 3, 4, 5, 6
   b. 1, 3, 2, 4, 5, 6
   c. 3, 2, 4, 5, 6
   d. 1, 4, 5, 6

2. Jill is alarmed! She cannot see the files in the root folder of the C drive with Windows Explorer. Some of these files are operating system files. She points out a second problem. There are some files in the root folder of the C drive that do not have extensions. You open the Folder Options applet in Control Panel. Which advanced settings will solve Jill's problems?

   a. Select the Display the full file name and extensions check box.
   b. Select the Display the full path in title bar check box.
   c. Select the Show hidden files and folders option button.
   d. Deselect the Hide file extensions for known file types check box.
   e. Deselect the Hide protected operating system files check box.

LAB 6.2 SCHEDULE A TASK

Objectives

The goal of this lab is to create a scheduled task so that it runs or executes at a time that is most convenient for you. For instance, you can schedule a backup program to run each night at 2:00 a.m. Or, you can create a scheduled task to open a Word document at noon each Wednesday. When the document opens, you are ready to type your weekly progress report for your boss. After completing this lab, you will be able to:

➤ Run a Control Panel applet

➤ View the Display Options

➤ Create a scheduled task

Materials Required

This lab will require the following:

➤ Access as an administrator to a computer with Windows 2000 Server

Estimated completion time: **30 minutes**

ACTIVITY

1. You should be logged on to your computer as an administrator. Click **Start**, point to **Settings**, click **Control Panel**, and then double-click **Scheduled Tasks**.

2. Double-click **Add Scheduled Task** to open the Scheduled Task Wizard.

3. Click **Next**.

4. Scroll and then click **Calculator**. Click **Next**.

5. Click **One time only**, and then click **Next**.

6. Click minutes in **Start Time**. Advance the minute setting by three minutes. Click **Next**.

7. Type the password for the indicated user account. Retype the password. Click **Next**.

8. Click **Finish**, and then wait for the Calculator to appear.

9. **Close** all open windows. Remain logged on as the administrator for the next lab.

Certification Objectives

Objectives for Microsoft Exam 70-215: Installing, Configuring, and Administering Microsoft Windows 2000 Server:

➤ Manage and optimize availability of system and user data

➤ Recover system and user data

Review Questions

1. Brian and Lillie have a bet on the sequence of steps to set up a scheduled task. They ask you to settle the bet by providing the correct sequence. Indicate the correct sequence of steps to execute after the Scheduled Task Wizard starts.

    1. Select the time frame to run the program.
    2. Select the program to run.
    3. Enter the time and date.
    4. Type and retype password.
    5. Select Finish.

    a. 2, 1, 3, 4, 5
    b. 1, 2, 3, 4, 5
    c. 1, 2, 4, 3, 5
    d. 2, 1, 4, 3, 5

2. Peter must run a program called runup at noon and at 6:00 p.m. Which solution will accomplish the task for Peter?

    a. Schedule a task with the twice-a-day option and enter two times.

    b. Schedule a task with the daily option and enter two times.

    c. Schedule a daily task at noon.

    d. Schedule a daily task at 6:00 p.m.

LAB 6.3 SET SYSTEM PERFORMANCE OPTIONS

Objectives

The goal of this lab is to view and set system performance options. You can configure two performance options in Windows 2000 Server: assign more processor resources to the foreground program to improve responsiveness, and adjust the size of the paging file to accommodate more robust applications. After completing this lab, you will be able to:

➤ Run a Control Panel applet

➤ View the System General Options

➤ View the System Performance Options

➤ Set the Application Response

➤ Set the Paging File Size

Materials Required

This lab will require the following:

➤ Access as an administrator to a computer with Windows 2000 Server

Estimated completion time: **30 minutes**

ACTIVITY

1. You should be logged on to your computer as an administrator. Click **Start**, point to **Settings**, click **Control Panel**, and then double-click **System**.

2. Click the **General** tab. Locate and record the amount of RAM memory: _____.

3. Click the **Advanced** Tab.

4. Click **Performance Options**.

5. Click the **Help** button in the upper-right corner of the dialog box, and then click **Applications**. Read the Help message.

6. Click the **Help** button again, and then click **Background services**. Read the Help message. Click on the Help message pop-up text box to close the message.

7. Click **Change**.

The recommended minimum paging file size is one and one-half times the RAM memory on the computer. The maximum paging file size is three times the installed RAM memory, or twice the minimum paging file size.

8. Click the drive that contains the paging file. Click the **Initial size (MB)** text box. Enter a value that is one and one-half times the RAM memory on your computer. Figure 6-3 shows paging file settings for a computer with 128 MB of RAM memory.

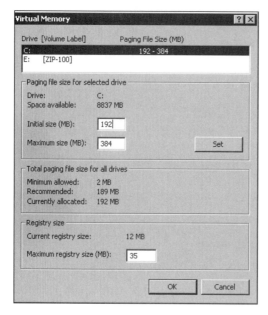

Figure 6-3   Paging file settings for a computer with 128 MB of RAM memory

The paging file cannot be placed on removable media. The ZIP-100 drive in Figure 6-3 would not be a suitable choice for the paging file.

9. Click the **Maximum size (MB)** text box. Enter a value that is three times the RAM memory on your computer.

10. Click **Set** to set the paging file size.

The location and size of the paging file can greatly affect performance. Placing the paging file on a separate, fast, low-use drive can boost performance. While the initial paging file size of one and one-half times the RAM memory on the computer is adequate for file and print servers, you should set the size of your paging file to two or two and one-half times the amount of RAM memory for application servers.

11. Click **OK**.

12. Click **OK**, and then click **OK** again.

13. **Close** all open windows. Remain logged on as the administrator for the next lab.

Certification Objectives

Objectives for Microsoft Exam 70–215: Installing, Configuring, and Administering Microsoft Windows 2000 Server:

➤ Manage and optimize availability of system and user data

Review Questions

1. For a Pentium III computer with 256 MB of RAM memory, indicate the recommended amount of initial and maximum paging file sizes for a Windows 2000 server. (Choose up to two correct answers.)
   a. 256 MB
   b. 384 MB
   c. 512 MB
   d. 768 MB

2. Brian is running a foreground application on a Windows 2000 server. Brian commented to Lillie that the Application Response was slow. Lillie stated that she could fix the problem. What did Lillie do to correct Brian's problem?
   a. Set the Application Response to true with the Registry Editor.
   b. Click Background Services in Application Response.
   c. Click Applications in Application Response.
   d. Move the Application Response slider in Performance Boost.

3. Jose is concerned about optimizing the paging file on his application server that has 512 MB of RAM memory. He asks you to review his plans for the reallocation of the paging file. Which of the following would you recommend?
   a. Create a initial paging file size of 768MB.
   b. Place the paging file on the same physical hard drive as Windows 2000 Server to optimize access to the Dynamic Link Library in the Windows 2000 operating system.
   c. Place the paging file on a physical hard drive that does not contain the Windows 2000 Server operating system.
   d. Create a initial paging file size of 1 GB.

Lab 6.4 Review Resources with Device Manager

Objectives

The goal of this lab is to view resources with the Device Manager. The Device Manager is the key tool to investigate and resolve hardware problems. The Device Manager can be used to quickly get an overview of the resources on a computer. This tool is especially helpful when you work on a server in your organization that you did not configure. After completing this lab, you will be able to:

➤ Run a Control Panel applet

➤ View the status of a device

➤ View the resource settings for a device

➤ View the potential conflicts for a device

➤ Select the Device Manager views

➤ View devices by type

➤ View resources by type

Materials Required

This lab will require the following:

➤ Access as an administrator to a computer with Windows 2000 Server

Estimated completion time: **30 minutes**

Activity

1. You should be logged on to your computer as an administrator. Click **Start**, point to **Settings**, click **Control Panel**, and then double-click **System**.

2. Click the **Hardware** tab, and then click **Device Manager.**

3. Observe the devices that are displayed by Device Manager. Expand **Display adapters**, right-click a display adapter, and then click **Properties**. Read the information on the **General** tab, especially the information on the Device status.

4. Click the **Resources** tab, view the Resource settings scroll box, view the Conflicting device list for potential device conflicts, and then click **Cancel.**

5. Click the **View** menu, and then click **Devices by type** to observe the devices on your computer.

6. Click the **View** menu, and then click **Resources by type** to observe the allocation of resources on your computer.

7. Expand the **Direct memory access (DMA)** entry in the directory. Review the use of DMAs on your computer.

8. Expand the **Input/Output(IO)** entry. Review the use of IO on your computer.

9. Expand the **Interrupt Request (IRQ)** entry. Review the use of IRQs on your computer.

 As a general rule, ISA bus devices must be assigned unique IRQs. PCI bus devices can share IRQs.

10. Expand the **Memory** entry. Review the memory allocations on your computer.

11. Close the **Device Manager** window.

12. Click **Cancel**, and then **close** any open windows.

13. Remain logged on as administrator.

Certification Objectives

Objectives for Microsoft Exam 70-215: Installing, Configuring, and Administering Microsoft Windows 2000 Server:

➤ Configure hardware devices

➤ Troubleshoot problems with hardware

Review Questions

1. Jill tries to remember the steps to determine if her network adapter is working properly. She is not sure of the exact sequence of steps. Can you help her? Indicate the correct steps and the correct sequence.

   1. Start the System applet in Control Panel.
   2. Click the Hardware tab and click Device Manager.
   3. Click View.
   4. Right-click the network adapter and click Properties.
   5. Expand Network Adapters.
   6. Read the Device status on the General tab.
   7. Click the Resources tab and view the Resource settings and Conflicting device list.

   a. 1, 2, 3, 4, 5, 6, 7
   b. 1, 2, 5, 4, 6, 7
   c. 2, 1, 3, 5, 4, 6, 7
   d. 2, 1, 4, 5, 3, 6, 7

2. Janet's boss gives her an assignment to add a sound card to the Security Alarm computer. A sound card will alert the guard on duty when a security breach is reported. She locates a box in the storeroom with a legacy sound card. She turns to the page in the manual that has the sound card resource requirements. Here are the requirements for the card:

IRQ 5

I/O 0330

DMA 01

Which resources should Janet check to ensure that the legacy sound card can be installed? (Choose all that apply.)

a. Direct Memory Access (DMA)

b. Input/Output (IO)

c. Interrupt Request (IRQ)

d. Memory

e. Audio Codes

LAB 6.5 USE CONFIGURE YOUR SERVER WIZARD

Objectives

The goal for this lab is to create a shared folder on your Windows 2000 server with the Configure Your Server Wizard. As a network administrator, you will set up file sharing, which allows other computers on a network to access resources on your computer. You will provide a share name for the folder that contains the files to be accessed over the network. With the Computer Management tool, you will manage the created shares on your server.

Share permissions set the allowable actions available for a shared folder. By default, everyone with access to the network has access to the folder. With NTFS volumes, you can use folder permissions to further constrain actions within the share. With FAT volumes, share permissions provide the only controls. After completing this lab, you will be able to:

➤ Launch the Configure Your Server Wizard

➤ Review the tasks supported by the Configure Your Server Wizard

➤ Create a shared folder with the Shared Folder Wizard

➤ Launch Computer Management

➤ Review the Shared Folder Properties

➤ Review share permissions and NTFS permissions

Materials Required

This lab will require the following:

➤ Access as an administrator to a computer with Windows 2000 Server.

➤ A disk volume formatted with NTFS

Estimated completion time: **60 minutes**

ACTIVITY

6

1. You should be logged on to your computer as an administrator. Click **Start**, point to **Programs**, point to **Administrative Tools**, and then click **Configure Your Server**.

2. Click **File Server** in the left pane. To discover the tasks for the File Server Wizard, read the text in the right pane.

3. Repeat Step 2 for the remaining wizards.

4. Click **File Server** in the left pane, and then click **Start the Shared Folder Wizard** in the right pane to start the wizard to create a shared folder.

5. Refer to Figure 6-4. Click **Browse**, click **Local Disk (C:)** (note that you also can click a volume formatted with NTFS and that your system might use a different drive letter), click the **New Folder** button, and then type *FolderFML* (where *F* is the first initial, *M* is the middle initial, and *L* is the last name for the user) in the **New Folder** text box.

Figure 6-4   Creating a shared folder

6. Click the *FolderFML* created in Step 3, click **OK**, type *ShareFML* in the Share name text box, type *Shared data for FML* in the Share description text box, and then click **Next**.

7. Because share permissions are important to the integrity of your administrative control over the network, review the basic share permissions. Then, click **All users have full control**, click **Finish**, click **No** to the message box, and then close the **Configure Your Server** window.

8. Click **Start**, point to **Programs**, point to **Administrative Tools**, and then click **Computer Management**.

9. Expand **System Tools**, expand **Shared Folders**, click **Shares**, and then review the shares for your server.

10. Locate the *ShareFML* folder, right-click the *ShareFML* folder, click **Properties**, and then review the shared path information that you entered in Step 7.

11. To review the share and NTFS permissions, click the **Share Permissions** tab, click the **Everyone** group, review the share permissions, click the **Security** tab, click the **Everyone** group, review the NTFS permissions, and then click **Cancel**.

12. Close the **Computer Management** window.

13. Log off your computer, and then shut down the computer.

Certification Objectives

Objectives for Microsoft Exam 70-215: Installing, Configuring, and Administering Microsoft Windows 2000 Server:

➤ Monitor, configure, troubleshoot, and control security on files and folders

➤ Monitor, configure, troubleshoot, and control access to files and folders in a shared folder

➤ Manage and optimize availability of system state and user data

Review Questions

1. Paul and Tony discover that Windows 2000 Server has the Configure Your Server Wizard. They ask you what tasks can be completed with this wizard. Which of the following will you discuss with Paul and Tony?
   a. Share a folder for access through the network.
   b. Set up a network printer for access through the network.
   c. Configure display devices on your server.
   d. Set up DHCP or DNS services on the network.
   e. Set up a Web server.

2. Barrett and Carolyn discuss the steps to create and share a folder on the network. Barrett provides what he perceives to be the prospective steps. They ask you for the proper sequence of steps. In what order should you execute which of the following steps to create and share a folder?

   1. Launch the Configure Your Server Wizard.
   2. Select Networking.
   3. Select File Server.
   4. Start the Shared Folder Wizard.
   5. Locate the folder and create a share name.
   6. Click Browse to locate the drive for the folder.
   7. Click New Folder and type the folder name.
   8. Click Finish.
   a. 1, 2, 3, 4, 6, 7, 5, 8
   b. 1, 3, 4, 6, 7, 5, 8
   c. 1, 2, 4, 6, 7, 5, 8
   d. 1, 2, 3, 4, 7, 6, 5, 8

3. Maria tries to recall which items can be reviewed using the Shares option for the Shared Folders with the Computer Management tool. Which items can be reviewed for a shared folder?
   a. FAT permissions for the files in the folder
   b. share permissions for the folder
   c. the share name on the network
   d. a comment describing the share
   e. the path on the local server

6

CONFIGURING SERVER STORAGE, BACKUP, AND PERFORMANCE OPTIONS

Labs included in this chapter

➤ Lab 7.1 Install the Disk Management Snap-In

➤ Lab 7.2 Manage a Logical Partition

➤ Lab 7.3 Convert a Basic Disk to a Dynamic Disk (Optional Lab)

➤ Lab 7.4 Manage a Simple Volume

➤ Lab 7.5 Create a Mounted Drive

➤ Lab 7.6 Back up a Folder to a File

Microsoft MCSE Exam #70-215 Objectives	
Objective	Lab
Upgrade a server from Windows NT 4.0	7.3
Optimize disk performance	7.1
Recover systems and user data	7.1, 7.6
Monitor, configure, and troubleshoot disks and volumes	7.1, 7.2, 7.3, 7.4, 7.5
Recover from disk failures	7.1, 7.6

LAB 7.1 INSTALL THE DISK MANAGEMENT SNAP-IN

Objectives

The goal of this lab is to install the Disk Management snap-in into the Microsoft Management Console (MMC). Disk Management is a graphical tool for managing disk storage. With Disk Management, you can manage the disks on your servers. The MMC is a container for management tools such as Disk Management.

The MMC consists of a window divided into two panes. The left pane shows the items that are available in a given console. The right pane contains the details pane. The details pane can display many types of program information including graphics, charts, tables, and columns. As you click different items in the left pane, the information in the details pane changes.

After a console is configured, you will want to save the console configuration file (.MSC) on the desktop. This will speed future access to the console. After completing this lab, you will be able to:

➤ Launch the Microsoft Management Console (MMC)

➤ Add the Disk Management snap-in to the MMC

➤ Save the MMC configuration file on the desktop

Materials Required

This lab will require the following:

➤ Access as an administrator to a computer with Windows 2000 Server

Activity Background

Disk Management is a tool for managing hard disks. With Disk Management, you can create volumes, format volumes with file systems, initialize disks, and create fault-tolerant disk systems.

Estimated completion time: **30 minutes**

ACTIVITY

1. Begin this lab with your computer turned on and the desktop visible on the monitor. Click **Start**, click **Run**, type **MMC**, and then click **OK**.

2. Click **Console**, click **Add/Remove Snap-in**, and then click **Add**.

3. Click **Disk Management**, and then click **Add**.

4. Click **Finish**, click **Close**, and then click **OK**.

5. Click **Console**, click **Save As**, and then click the **Save in** drop-down list. Click **Desktop**.

6. Click the **File name** text box, type **DiskMgt**, and then click **Save**.

7. Click **Console**, and then click **Exit**.

Certification Objectives

Objectives for Microsoft Exam 70-215: Installing, Configuring, and Administering Microsoft Windows 2000 Server:

➤ Monitor, configure, and troubleshoot disks and volumes

Review Questions

1. Which of the following tasks can be accomplished using the Disk Management tool?
   a. creation of volumes
   b. formatting of volumes with file systems
   c. initialization of disks
   d. creation of fault-tolerant volumes
   e. all of the above

2. Brian and Lillie discuss the MMC. They ask you for clarification on several characteristics of the MMC. Which items will you include in your discussion?
   a. The left pane contains a list of the items in the console.
   b. The left and right panes are coordinated. Clicking in the right pane affects the items displayed in the left pane.
   c. The right pane contains the details for the selected item.
   d. The details pane displays graphics, charts, and tables.

LAB 7.2 MANAGE A LOGICAL PARTITION

Objectives

The goal of this lab is to create an extended partition. You can create up to four partitions in the free space on a physical hard disk. One of these four partitions, if disk space allows, can be an extended partition. You can use the free space in the extended partition to create multiple logical drives. To avoid changing the letters of drives, do not create additional primary partitions after you create the extended partition. By changing the letters of drives, you run the risk of losing access to applications that depend on a fixed drive location. After completing this lab, you will be able to:

➤ Launch the MMC configuration file from the desktop

➤ Create an extended partition

➤ Create a logical drive

➤ Remove a logical drive

➤ Remove an extended partition

Materials Required

This lab will require the following:

➤ Access as an administrator to a computer with Windows 2000 Server and the following: a basic disk with raw disk space for the allocation of an extended partition, no more than three primary partitions, and no extended partitions

Estimated completion time: **30 minutes**

ACTIVITY

1. You should be logged on to your computer as an administrator. To launch MMC, double-click **DiskMgt** on the desktop, and then click **Disk Management (Local)** to view the partitions on your computer.

Use the color-coded legend in Disk Management to determine the disk allocations.

2. Review current drive settings. In particular, look for unallocated space

3. Right-click the **Unallocated area** on the image of the disk allocations, click **Create Partition**, read the welcome screen, and then click **Next**.

4. Click **Extended Partition** and read the description. Click **Next**.

5. Review the amount of disk space to use, and then click **Next**.

6. Click **Finish**.

7. Now that you have created an extended partition, you will create a logical drive. Right-click **Free Space in Extended Partition**. (The legend indicates the color for the extended partition.) Click **Create Logical Drive**, and then click **Next**.

8. Click **Next** to create the logical drive.

9. Type **100** in the Amount of disk space to use text box, and then click **Next**.

10. Retain the default drive letter by clicking **Next**, click the **File system** drop-down arrow, and then click **FAT**.

11. Click **Next**, and then click **Finish**.

12. Wait for the partition to be formatted, and then right-click the logical drive you just created. Click **Delete Logical Drive**, and then click **Yes** to delete the logical drive. (While completing this step, click **OK** to any message boxes that appear.)

13. Right-click the extended partition you created earlier, and then click **Delete Partition**.

14. Click **Yes** to delete the free space.

15. Leave the Disk Management Console open for the next lab.

Certification Objectives

Objectives for Microsoft Exam 70-215: Installing, Configuring, and Administering Microsoft Windows 2000 Server:

➤ Monitor, configure, and troubleshoot disks and volumes

Review Questions

1. Brian and Lillie view the disk space allocation on the hard drive of a server. Lillie is not sure how to identify the various types of allocations. Which of the following could appear in the legend bar in Disk Management?
   a. Primary partition
   b. Secondary partition
   c. Extended partition
   d. Logical drive
   e. Free space

2. Disk Management can apply a number of file systems to a partition. Which file system formats are supported?
   a. FAT
   b. FAT32
   c. HPFS
   d. NTFS

3. John is planning the disk allocations for his home computer. He wants to support the following operating systems for the courses at Local U:
   Windows 98
   Windows NT 4.0
   Windows 2000 Professional
   Windows 2000 Server

   In addition, he wants to set up a common data area to store his research papers.

   He provides you with a diagram of his disk allocations. You review the diagram and discover these disk allocations:

   Drive C: Primary partition of 500 MB for Windows 98 as FAT32
   Drive D: Primary partition of 500 MB for Windows NT as FAT
   Drive E: Primary partition of 1 GB for Windows 2000 Professional as NTFS
   Drive F: Primary partition of 1 GB for Windows 2000 Server as NTFS
   Drive G: Primary partition of 5 GB for common data as FAT32

Indicate the outcome for John's diagram:

a. With Disk Management, the limit of four primary partitions can be exceeded successfully by using the primary partition consolidate option.

b. With Disk Management, there is no limit to the number of primary partitions, and the allocations will be successful.

c. With Disk Management, the limit of four primary partitions can be exceeded successfully by using the primary partition combine option.

d. With Disk Management, only four primary partitions can be allocated, and the allocations will fail.

LAB 7.3 CONVERT A BASIC DISK TO A DYNAMIC DISK (OPTIONAL LAB)

Objectives

The goal of this lab is to convert a basic disk to a dynamic disk. A dynamic disk is a physical disk that contains dynamic volumes created using Disk Management.

With dynamic disks, you can accomplish administrative tasks without interrupting your users. For example, you can create, extend, or mirror a volume without restarting the system. You can also add a new disk without restarting. As an added bonus, you need not wait for most configuration changes to take effect when you use a dynamic disk.

To set up a new fault-tolerant disk system, you must use dynamic disks. If you plan to create volume, stripe, mirrors, or stripe sets with parity, you must use dynamic disks. This lab is optional because you cannot convert a dynamic disk back to a basic disk without losing the contents of the dynamic disk! After completing this lab, you will be able to:

➤ Convert a basic disk to a dynamic disk

Materials Required

This lab will require the following:

➤ Access as an administrator to a computer with Windows 2000 Server. The server must have a basic disk available to convert to a dynamic disk. In addition, the basic disk must have 1 MB of free space at the end of the disk.

Estimated completion time: **30 minutes**

ACTIVITY

1. Your computer should have the Disk Management Console open and all other programs closed.

2. To select the basic disk to be upgraded to dynamic, right-click the **Basic** target button, which contains a disk symbol and the word Basic.

You cannot change the dynamic volumes back to basic disks without removing all the volumes.

3. Click **Upgrade to Dynamic Disk**, verify the disk to be upgraded, and then click **OK**.

4. Confirm the disk selected for the upgrade, and then click **Upgrade**.

5. Read the information regarding the upgrade, and then click **Yes**.

6. Read the information about file systems being force dismounted, and then click **Yes**.

7. If the Save Console Settings message box appears, click **No**.

8. Click **OK** to permit the first system restart.

9. Click **End Now** to close the Disk Management Console. The system will restart.

10. Log on to the system as **administrator**.

11. Click **Yes** to restart the system for the second time.

12. Double-click the **DiskMgt** icon on the desktop.

13. Review the changes in the Disk Management Console. Specifically, note that the basic disk was converted to a dynamic disk, and the partitions are now simple volumes.

14. Right-click the **Dynamic** disk button, and then click **Reactivate Disk** to remove the yellow explanation mark. Leave the console open for the next lab.

Certification Objectives

Objectives for Microsoft Exam 70-215: Installing, Configuring, and Administering Microsoft Windows 2000 Server:

➤ Monitor, configure, and troubleshoot disks and volumes

Review Questions

1. You prepare to talk to your boss about the advantages of dynamic disks. Which of the following will be in your list of selling points?

a. They manage disk allocations without forcing a restart of the system.

b. They are required to set up a new RAID-5.

c. They can be converted to basic disks without losing data.

d. They extend volume sizes to increase space for additional files.

2. Bob and Jill discuss the conversion of basic disks to dynamic disks. Jill listed the steps to create a mount point, but they need you to supply the correct order for the steps.

1. Right-click the disk to convert.
2. Click Upgrade.
3. Click Upgrade to Dynamic Disk.
4. Restart the system.

Which of the following is the correct order of the steps?
   a. 1, 3, 2, 4
   b. 1, 2, 3, 4
   c. 1, 3, 2, 4, 4
   d. 1, 2, 4, 2

LAB 7.4 MANAGE A SIMPLE VOLUME

Objectives

The goal of this lab is to create a simple volume on a dynamic disk. A simple volume is part of a physical disk that appears as a physically separate unit.

A simple volume is made up of disk space on a single physical disk. You can extend a simple volume within the same disk, or onto additional disks. If you extend a simple volume across multiple disks, it becomes a spanned volume. If you lose a portion of an extended or spanned volume, data on the remaining portions is lost. For example, deleting a portion of the extended volume removes the remaining portions of the extended volume.

When you have only one dynamic disk, you can create simple volumes. (If you had multiple dynamic disks, you could create fault-tolerant volumes.) As you need additional space for more files, the volume can be extended. After completing this lab, you will be able to:

➤ Launch the MMC file from the desktop

➤ Create a simple volume

➤ Extend a simple volume

➤ Remove a simple volume

Materials Required

This lab will require the following:

➤ Access as an administrator to a computer with Windows 2000 Server. The server must have available space on a dynamic disk. Free space of 500MB is adequate.

Estimated completion time: **30 minutes**

ACTIVITY

1. Your computer should have the Disk Management Console open and all other programs closed. Double-click the **DiskMgt** icon on the desktop. Click **Disk Management (Local)** to view partitions.

2. Right-click in the unallocated area, and then click **Create Volume**.

3. Read the Welcome to Create Volume Wizard information, and then click **Next**.

4. Verify that **Simple volume** is selected. Read the description, and then click **Next**.

5. Type **500** for the selected disk, and then click **Next**.

6. Click **Next** to assign the next drive letter.

7. Verify that **NTFS** as File system to use is selected. Click **Next**.

8. Review the choices, and then click **Finish**.

9. Wait for volume to format.

To view the formatting progress, place your mouse over the volume allocation that you created.

10. Right-click the **New Volume**, click **Extend Volume**, and then click **Next**.

11. Type **500** for the selected disk, click **Next**, and then click **Finish**.

12. Review the Disk Management Console. Verify that both volumes have the same drive letter.

13. Right-click the **New Volume**, click **Delete Volume**, and then click **Yes** to delete the volumes.

14. Review the Disk Management Console and verify that the volumes were removed.

Certification Objectives

Objectives for Microsoft Exam 70-215: Installing, Configuring, and Administering Microsoft Windows 2000 Server:

➤ Monitor, configure, and troubleshoot disks and volumes

➤ Recover from disk failures

Review Questions

1. You are creating a list of facts about simple volumes. Which of the following will be included in your list?
   a. A volume is part of a physical disk.
   b. A volume requires a dynamic disk.
   c. A volume requires a basic disk.
   d. A volume can be extended.

2. George discovered Disk Management. He developed a plan to implement volumes on dynamic disks. He mapped out the disk allocations in Table 7-1.

Table 7-1   Disk Allocations

Disk0	Vol0 NTFS	Vol0 NTFS	Vol1 NTFS	Vol2 NTFS
Disk1	Vol1 NTFS	Vol2 NTFS	Free Space	

Which of the following are your observations about George's plan?
   a. The simple volumes can be extended.
   b. The loss of a single portion results in a total loss of volume.
   c. The simple volumes can be spanned across disks.
   d. The simple volumes can be used only with basic disks.
   e. The simple volumes formatted as FAT can be extended.

LAB 7.5 CREATE A MOUNTED DRIVE

Objectives

The goal of this lab is to create a mounted drive. You can use mounted drives to access more than 26 drives on your computer.

Mounted drives free drive letters that you can then use for network access. For instance, when you mount a local drive on an empty folder on an NTFS volume, Windows 2000 Server assigns a drive path to the drive rather than a drive letter. So, if, for example, you have a CD-ROM drive with the drive letter D, and an NTFS-formatted volume with the drive letter C, you could mount the CD-ROM drive at the empty folder C:\CD-ROM, and then access the CD-ROM drive directly through the path C:\CD-ROM. Then, you can remove the drive letter D.

With mounted drives, you gain the flexibility to manage data storage based on your work environment and system requirements. For example, you can make the C:\Temp folder a mounted drive to provide additional disk space for temporary files on another drive. After completing this lab, you will be able to:

➤ Launch the MMC configuration file from the desktop

➤ Create a mounted drive

➤ Use a mounted drive to view the contents of a drive

Materials Required

This lab will require the following:

➤ Access as an administrator to a computer with Windows 2000 Server. The server must have multiple partitions or volumes using the NTFS file system.

7

Estimated completion time: **30 minutes**

ACTIVITY

1. Your computer should have the Disk Management Console open and all other programs closed. Double-click the **DiskMgt** icon on the desktop, if necessary. Click **Disk Management (Local)** to view the drives.

Your instructor will help you decide which drive to mount. For reference, we will call this the "first" drive. Your instructor will help you select another drive for the new folder; we will call this the "second" drive.

2. Right-click the **first drive**, and click **Change Drive Letter and Paths**.

3. Click **Add**. Your screen should resemble Figure 7-1.

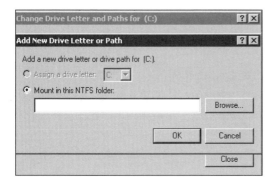

Figure 7-1   Adding the drive path

4. Click **Browse**, click the **second drive**, click **New Folder**, and then type **MapFirst**. Your screen should resemble Figure 7-2. Click **OK**.

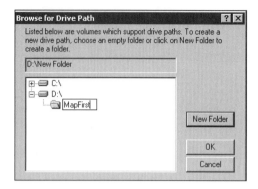

Figure 7-2   Result of adding the drive path

5. Click **OK**.

6. Right-click on the **second drive**, and then click **Explore**.

7. Double-click the **MapFirst** icon. You should see the contents of the first drive. (If you do not, contact your instructor.) Close the **Explorer** window.

8. Right-click the **first drive**, click **Change Drive Letter and Path**, click the drive letter and path you created in Step 2, and then click **Remove**.

9. Click **Yes** to confirm the removal of the mount point.

10. Right-click the **second drive**, click **Explore**, right-click the **MapFirst** folder, click **Delete**, and then click **Yes** to confirm deletion. **Close** all windows.

Certification Objectives

Objectives for Microsoft Exam 70-215: Installing, Configuring, and Administering Microsoft Windows 2000 Server:

➤ Monitor, configure, and troubleshoot disks and volumes

➤ Optimize disk performance

Review Questions

1. Lillie and Brian discuss the creation of mount points. Lillie listed the steps to create a mount point, but they need you to supply the correct order for the steps.

   1. Right-click the partition or volume to mount.
   2. Click Change Drive Letter and Paths.
   3. Click Add.
   4. Click New Folder.
   5. Click Browse.

Which of the following is the correct order of the steps?

a. 1, 3, 2, 4, 5

b. 1, 2, 3, 5, 4

c. 1, 4, 2, 3, 5

d. 1, 4, 5, 2, 3

2. Joan considers implementing mount points to provide easier access for her users. Currently, she has CD-ROM drives that contain the monthly financials at drive G, and the annual financials at drive H. Space is limited on the D drive. She installed a new drive on the server. She has set the following goals for her implementation:

1. Eliminate the G drive letter used by the first CD-ROM drive
2. Eliminate the H drive letter used by the second CD-ROM drive
3. Provide additional drive space for the D:\TEMP folder
4. Move a folder named Application to a new disk

Joan proposed the following solution:

1. Mount the first CD-ROM drive through the path D:\MONTHLY.
2. Mount the second CD-ROM drive through the path D:\ANNUAL.
3. Clear the temporary files for D:\TEMP.
4. Move the application files to the new disk and make the D:\APPLICATION folder a mounted drive.

Which of the goals will be achieved?

a. The first goal will be met.

b. The second goal will be met.

c. The third goal will be met.

d. The fourth goal will be met.

e. No goals will be met.

LAB 7.6 BACK UP A FOLDER TO A FILE

Objectives

The goal of this lab is to practice backing up a folder. As a network administrator, you will be backing up user and system data on a regular schedule.

The reasons for backing up are varied. For example, you can use backup to create a duplicate copy of the data on your hard disk, and then archive the data on another hard disk or a tape. If the original data on your hard disk is accidentally erased or overwritten, or your hard disk crashes, you can easily restore the data from the archived copy. After completing this lab, you will be able to:

➤ Launch the Backup program

➤ Back up the Documents and Settings folder for the administrator's account to a file

Materials Required

This lab will require the following:

➤ Access as an administrator to a computer running Windows 2000 Server

Estimated completion time: **30 minutes**

ACTIVITY

1. Begin this lab with your computer turned on and the desktop visible on the monitor. You should be logged on to your computer as an administrator. Click **Start**, point to **Accessories**, point to **System Tools**, and then click **Backup**.

 Backup provides you with a tree view of the drives, files, and folders that are on your computer. You can use the tree view to select the files and folders that you want to back up.

2. Click the **Backup** tab. Expand **C:**, and then expand the **Documents and Settings** folder. Click the **Administrator** check box, and then click the **Administrator** folder. Your screen should resemble Figure 7-3.

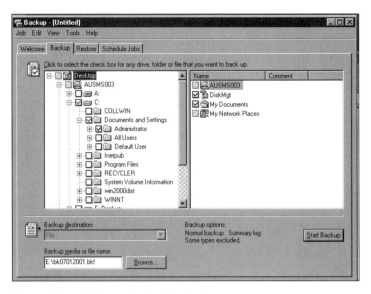

Figure 7-3   Folder selected for backup

3. Click **Browse**, click the **Look in** drop-down arrow, and then click the drive that you will use for backup.

When you back up data to a file, you must designate a file name and a location for the file to be saved. You can save a backup file to a hard disk or a removable disk, such as a Zip drive.

4. Type **bk*yyyymmdd*** (where *yyyy* is the year, *mm* is the month, and *dd* is the day) in the File name text box. Your screen should resemble Figure 7-4. Click **Open**.

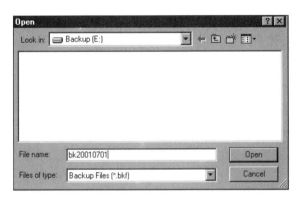

Figure 7-4   Location selected for backup file

5. Click **Start Backup**.

6. Review the backup job information, as shown in Figure 7-5, and then click **Start Backup**.

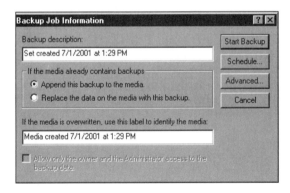

Figure 7-5   Sample backup job information memory

7. Wait for Backup to complete, and then review the completed backup progress.

8. Click **Report**, review the Backup log (look for the number of files backed up, Bytes, and Time). Click **File** on the menu bar, and then click **Exit**.

If files are open, the Backup program cannot access the files. The Backup log will indicate which files were open.

9. Click **Close**, click **Job,** and then click **Exit**.

Certification Objectives

Objectives for Microsoft Exam 70–215: Installing, Configuring, and Administering Microsoft Windows 2000 Server:

➤ Monitor, configure, and troubleshoot disks and volumes

➤ Manage and optimize availability of system and user data

Review Questions

1. Backup can create an archive of a folder on which of the following?
   a. a tape drive
   b. a hard disk
   c. a removable disk
   d. a CD-ROM

2. Which of the following can be included in a backup?
   a. computers
   b. drives
   c. folders
   d. files

3. Lillie and Brian discuss the backup of folders. They ask you for the correct order of the steps involved. The steps are listed below:

   1. Launch the Backup program.
   2. Select the location for the Backup file.
   3. Select the drives, files, and folders to back up.
   4. Type the file name for Backup.
   5. Start Backup.

   Which of the following is the correct order of the steps?
   a. 1, 2, 3, 4, 5
   b. 1, 2, 3, 4, 5
   c. 1, 3, 2, 4, 5
   d. 1, 4, 5, 2, 3

CHAPTER EIGHT

MANAGING ACCOUNTS AND CLIENT CONNECTIVITY

Labs included in this chapter

➤ Lab 8.1 Set Audit Policy for User Account Changes

➤ Lab 8.2 Create and Test a Local User Account

➤ Lab 8.3 Manage a Local Account

➤ Lab 8.4 Create a Password Policy

➤ Lab 8.5 Create a Local Security Group Policy

➤ Lab 8.6 Reviewing the Security Log for User Account Changes

---

Microsoft MCSE Exam #70-215 Objectives

Objective	Lab
Configure and manage user profiles	8.2, 8.3
Install, configure and troubleshoot a virtual private network (VPN)	8.2
Configure, monitor, and troubleshoot remote acccess	8.2
Implement, configure, manage, and troubleshoot policies in a Windows 2000 environment	8.1, 8.2, 8.3, 8.4, 8.5, 8.6
Implement, configure, manage, and troubleshoot auditing	8.1, 8.6
Implement, configure, manage, and troubleshoot local accounts	8.1, 8.2, 8.3, 8.6
Implement, configure, manage, and troubleshoot Account Policy	8.4, 8.5, 8.6
Implement, configure, manage, and troubleshoot security by using the Security Configuration Tool Set	8.2

LAB 8.1 SET AUDIT POLICY FOR USER ACCOUNT CHANGES

Objective

The goal of this lab is to create an audit policy to track user account changes. Auditing is the best way to track changes to user accounts on your server. To set up audit policy, you must install the Group Policy snap-in. With Group Policy, you can manage the actions of the users for your server. In addition, you can use it to define the allowed actions and settings for users of your server.

In this lab, you will set up audit tracking, which enables you to keep a record of changes you make to user accounts in successive labs. After completing this lab, you will be able to:

➤ Launch the Microsoft Management Console (MMC)

➤ Add the Group Policy snap-in to the MMC

➤ Save the MMC file on the desktop

➤ Create an audit policy to track user account activity

Materials Required

This lab will require the following:

➤ Access as an administrator to a computer running Windows 2000 Member Server

Estimated completion time: **30 minutes**

ACTIVITY

1. Begin this lab with your computer turned on and the desktop visible on the monitor. You should be logged on as an administrator.

2. Click **Start**, click **Run**, type **MMC**, and then click **OK**.

3. Click **Console**, click **Add/Remove Snap-in**, click **Add**, click **Group Policy**, click **Add**, click **Finish**, click **Close**, and then click **OK**.

4. Click **Console**, click **Save As**, click the **Save in** drop-down arrow, click **Desktop**, click the **File name** text box, type **UserMgt**, and then click **Save**.

5. Expand **Local Computer Policy**, expand **Computer Configuration**, and then expand **Windows Settings**.

6. Expand **Security Settings**, expand **Local Policies**, and then click **Audit Policy** to view the audit policies in the right pane, as shown in Figure 8-1.

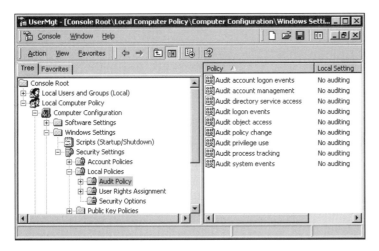

Figure 8-1   Viewing audit policies

7. Double-click **Audit logon events**, click **Failure**, and then click **OK**.

8. Double-click **Audit account management**, click **Success**, click **Failure**, and then click **OK**.

9. Remain logged on for the next lab with the Microsoft Management Console open.

Certification Objectives

Objectives for Microsoft Exam 70-215: Installing, Configuring, and Administering Microsoft Windows 2000 Server:

➤ Implement, configure, manage, and troubleshoot local accounts

➤ Implement, configure, manage, and troubleshoot auditing

Review Questions

1. Susan asks you about the capabilities of the Group Policy snap-in. Which of the following items will you discuss with Susan?

   a. The Group Policy snap-in provides a graphical administration tool.

   b. The Group Policy snap-in is added to the Microsoft Management Console.

   c. The Group Policy snap-in administers policies on a local server.

   d. The Group Policy snap-in administers policies on a domain controller.

2. You are learning to use the account management tools in Windows 2000 Server. You installed the Group Policy snap-in on your Windows 2000 member server. Which of the following would you select to record the changes that you will make during the creation and management of user accounts?

   a. Audit account logon attempts

   b. Audit account management failures

      c. Audit account management changes

      d. Audit account logon failures

LAB 8.2 CREATE AND TEST A LOCAL USER ACCOUNT

Objectives

The goal of this lab is to create a local user account. You can create local user accounts for each individual who wants to use resources on your server. These user accounts control access to your server. Controlling access is a day-to-day task for most network administrators.

You must install the snap-in for Local Users and Groups, a graphical tool for local users on your server. It manages users and groups of users for your server. You can create new users and groups, add users to groups, remove users from groups, disable user and group accounts, and reset passwords. After completing this lab, you will be able to:

➤ Launch the MMC file from the desktop

➤ Add the Local Users and Groups snap-in

➤ Add a user account with Local Users and Groups

➤ Add a user account to the Power Users group with Local Users and Groups

➤ Test the created user account

Materials Required

This lab will require the following:

➤ Access as an administrator to a computer running a Windows 2000 Member Server

Estimated completion time: **30 minutes**

ACTIVITY

1. You should still be logged on as you were at the end of Lab 8-1. If you logged out, you must log in and double-click the **UserMgt** icon on the desktop.

2. In the Microsoft Management Console, click **Console**, click **Add/Remove Snap-in**, click **Add**, and then click **Local Users and Groups**.

3. Click **Add**, click **Finish**, click **Close**, and then click **OK**.

4. Expand **Local Users and Groups (Local)**. Click the **Users** folder to display the existing user accounts in the right pane.

5. Click the **Action** menu, and then click **New User**.

6. Click the **User name** text box, type *LastnameFM* (where *F* is the first initial, *M* is the middle initial, and *Lastname* is the last name of the user), and then press **Tab**.

7. Type the full name of the user, and then press **Tab**.

8. Type a descriptive comment in the **Description** text box, and then press **Tab**.

9. Enter a password, press **Tab**, and then confirm the password.

Most network administrators will use the "password of the day" and type the same password for each user account created. When many accounts are added, the rhythm of typing the same password can increase productivity. This should only be done when the "user must change password at next logon" check box has been retained.

10. Make sure the **User must change password at next logon** check box is checked, as shown in Figure 8-2. Click **Create**, and then click **Close**.

8

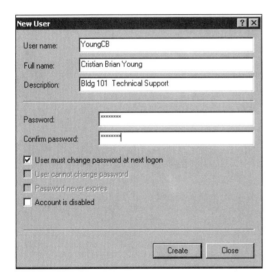

Figure 8-2   Entering a new user

11. Right-click *LastnameFM*. Click **Properties**.

12. Click the **Member Of** tab, and then click **Add**.

13. Click **Power Users**, click **Add**, click **OK**, click **Apply**, and then click **Close**.

14. Click **Console**, click **Exit**, and then click **Yes** to the message prompt.

15. Log off the system and log on again with the user account you just created in this series of steps, press **Tab**, type the **password** to the user account, and then click **OK**.

16. Read the logon message, and then click **OK**.

17. Create and enter a **password** that is at least six characters in length and that contains one capital letter, one number, and four lowercase characters. Press **Tab**, enter the **password** again as confirmation, and then click **OK**.

18. Read the message prompt, and then click **OK**.

19. Log off the system and log on again as the **administrator**. Remain logged on for the next lab.

Certification Objectives

Objectives for Microsoft Exam 70-215: Installing, Configuring, and Administering Microsoft Windows 2000 Server Objectives:

➤ Implement, configure, manage, and troubleshoot local accounts

➤ Implement, configure, manage, and troubleshoot account policy

➤ Implement, configure, manage, and troubleshoot auditing

Review Questions

1. Brian and Lillie discuss account-naming schemes. They created a list of user account names. Which names would be appropriate for a large organization?
   a. bluedart
   b. jonesj
   c. jonesjl
   d. jones_jeanette

2. John is designing a form for new users to request an account. Which items should be mandatory on the form?
   a. First name
   b. Middle initial
   c. Last name
   d. Building number
   e. Department
   f. Hire date

3. When completing the creation of a user account, you enter the "password of the day" and check the User must change password at next logon check box. After creating the account, you call the user. With the logon splash displayed on the Windows 2000 Professional computer, in what order will the user execute the following steps?
   1. Type the password provided.
   2. Type the User name provided.
   3. Create a new password.
   4. Type the new password, press Tab, and then retype the new password.

5. Read the "You are required to change your password at first logon" message.
   a. 1, 2, 3, 4, 5
   b. 2, 1, 5, 4
   c. 2, 1, 5, 3, 4
   d. 1, 2, 3, 5, 4

LAB 8.3 MANAGE A LOCAL ACCOUNT

Objectives

The goal of this lab is to manage a local user account. Many day-to-day activities for network administrators involve the management of user accounts. In addition to creating new users and adding new users to groups, you will be called upon to remove users from groups, disable user accounts, and reset passwords. After completing this lab, you will be able to:

➤ Launch the MMC file from the desktop

➤ Reset a password for a user account with Local Users and Groups

➤ Remove a user account from the Power Users group with Local Users and Groups

➤ Rename a user account with Local Users and Groups

➤ Disable, test, and re-enable the user account

Materials Required

This lab will require the following:

➤ Access as an administrator to a computer with Windows 2000 Member Server

➤ Completion of Lab 8.1 and Lab 8.2

Estimated completion time: **30 minutes**

ACTIVITY

1. You should still be logged on as you were at the end of Lab 8.2. If you logged out, you must log in as **administrator**. Double-click **UserMgt**, click **Local Users and Groups (Local)**, and then double-click the **Users** icon to see the existing user accounts in the right pane, as shown in Figure 8-3.

2. Right-click the user account created in Lab 8.3, click **Set Password**, type a **password** that contains seven characters (at least one capital letter, one number, one symbol, and four lowercase characters), and then press **Tab**.

3. Confirm the **password** by entering it again, click **OK**, and then click **OK** to the resulting message box.

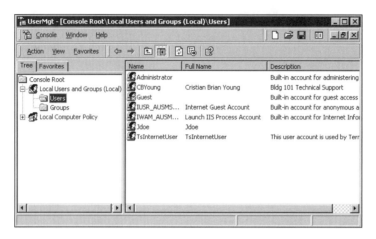

Figure 8-3   Existing user accounts

Note

If you get a message that the password was not confirmed, retype both passwords.

4. Click the **Groups** icon to see the existing user accounts in the right pane.

5. Double-click **Power Users**, click the user account created in Lab 8.2, click **Remove**, click **Apply**, and then click **Close**.

6. Click the **Users** icon to see the existing user accounts in the right pane, right-click the user account created in Lab 8.2, and then click **Rename**.

7. Rename the user account *FMLastname* (where *F* is the first initial, *M* is the middle initial, and *Lastname* is the last name of the user), and then click any white space to accept the new name.

8. Right-click the account you renamed in Step 7, and then click **Properties**.

9. Click **Account is disabled** to disable the account, click **Apply**, and then click **Close**.

10. Click **Console** on the menu bar, click **Exit**, and then click **Yes** to the message prompt.

11. Log off as the administrator, log on as the account you just renamed, press **Tab**, type the account password, and then click **OK**. You should see this message: Your account has been disabled. Please see your administrator.

12. Click **OK**, and then log on as the **administrator**.

13. Double-click **UserMgt**, double-click **Local Users and Groups (Local)**, and then double-click the **Users** icon to see the existing user accounts in the right pane.

14. Right-click the user account you renamed, click **Properties,** click **Account is disabled** to enable the account, click **Apply**, and then click **Close**.

15. Remain logged on for the next lab.

Certification Objectives

Objectives for Microsoft Exam 70-215: Installing, Configuring, and Administering Microsoft Windows 2000 Server:

➤ Implement, configure, manage, and troubleshoot local accounts

➤ Implement, configure, manage, and troubleshoot account policy

➤ Implement, configure, manage, and troubleshoot auditing

➤ Implement, configure, manage, and troubleshoot policies in a Windows 2000 environment

Review Questions

1. An employee at your company took a leave of absence. You're not sure whether the employee will return. What should you do for security purposes until a final decision is made?

    a. Lock out the user account.

    b. Disable the user account.

    c. Delete the user account.

    d. Rename the user account.

2. Brian and Lillie are having another routine discussion. They ask you to tell them about the password options when a new local user account is created. Which of these items will you point out?

    a. The user must change the password at the next logon.

    b. The user cannot change the password.

    c. The password never expires.

    d. The account is disabled.

    e. The account is locked out.

3. You created a new user with the Local Users and Groups snap-in. What is the default membership status when a user is added?

    a. the Guest group

    b. the Users group

    c. the Everyone group

    d. A new user account is not a member of any group until the account is added by an administrator.

LAB 8.4 CREATE A PASSWORD POLICY

Objectives

The goal of this lab is to create a password policy. Your task is to implement good computer security that includes the use of strong passwords for your network logon and the administrator account on your server. After completing this lab, you will be able to:

> ➤ Launch the MMC file from the desktop

> ➤ Create an effective password policy

> ➤ Set up a password policy using the Group Policy snap-in

Materials Required

This lab will require the following:

> ➤ Access as an administrator to a computer with Windows 2000 Member Server

> ➤ Completion of Lab 8.1

Activity Background

A good password should:

> ➤ be at least seven characters long.

> ➤ contain letters (uppercase and lowercase), numerals, and symbols.

> ➤ have at least one symbol character in the second through sixth position.

> ➤ be significantly different from prior passwords.

> ➤ not contain your name or user name.

> ➤ not be a common word or name.

Estimated completion time: **30 minutes**

ACTIVITY

1. You should still be logged on as you were at the end of Lab 8.3. If you logged out, you must log on and double-click the **UserMgt** icon on the desktop. Expand **Local Computer Policy**, expand **Computer Configuration**, and then expand **Windows Settings**.

Local Security Policy is only available on Windows 2000 computers that are not domain controllers. If the computer is a member of a domain, these settings may be overridden by policies received from the domain.

2. Expand **Security Settings**, expand **Account Policies**, and then click **Password Policy** to view the password policies in the right pane, as shown in Figure 8-4.

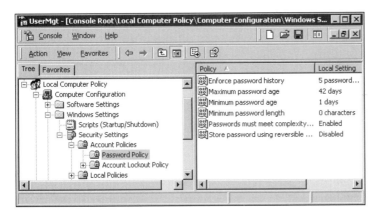

Figure 8-4   Viewing password policy

3. Double-click **Enforce password history**, review the effective and local policy settings, adjust the counter to **10**, and then click **OK**.

While Windows 2000 can store up to 24 passwords for each user, you will want to balance the password history with the minimum password age. For example, a password history of 10 coupled with a minimum password age of 10 will result in the user waiting over 100 days before reusing a password.

4. Double-click **Maximum password age**, review the effective and local policy settings, adjust the counter to **30**, and then click **OK**.

5. Double-click **Minimum password age**, review the effective and local policy settings, adjust the counter to **5** to keep users from immediately resetting the new password back to the previous one, and then click **OK**.

6. Double-click **Minimum password length**, review the effective and local policy settings, adjust the counter to **7**, and then click **OK**.

7. Double-click **Passwords must meet complexity requirements**, review the effective and local policy settings, click **Enabled**, and then click **OK**.

8. In the left pane, click **Account Lockout Policy** to view the policy in the right pane, as shown in Figure 8-5.

9. Double-click **Account lockout threshold**, review the effective and local policy settings, adjust the counter to **10**, and then click **OK**. If you see a message box about duration and counter settings, click **OK**.

8

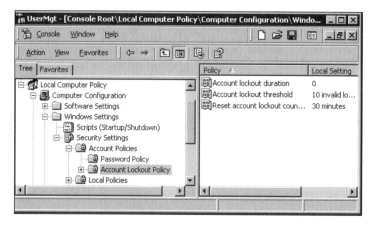

Figure 8-5   Account lockout policy

Account lockout threshold sets the number of logon attempts allowed before an account is locked out. A reasonable value is between 7 and 15. Such a value is low enough to thwart hackers while still allowing for user error.

10. Double-click **Account lockout duration**, review the effective and local policy settings, adjust the counter to **0**, and then click **OK**.

The best policy is to set the lockout duration to 0. This will lock the account and require the user to contact an administrator to unlock the account. At that time you can discuss the problem with the user.

11. Double-click **Reset account lockout counter after**, review the effective and local policy settings, adjust the counter to **30**, if necessary, and then click **OK**.

12. Remain logged on for the next lab.

Certification Objectives

Objectives for Microsoft Exam 70-215: Installing, Configuring, and Administering Microsoft Windows 2000 Server:

➤ Implement, configure, manage, and troubleshoot account policy

➤ Implement, configure, manage, and troubleshoot policies in a Windows 2000 environment

Review Questions

1. You and your peers discuss password policy. You write the examples that your peers contribute on the flip chart. Which of the examples are considered "strong" passwords?
   a. Pocket
   b. Pocket#3
   c. p##Ket3
   d. Pock#3

2. You are asked to explain the Account lockout threshold to a peer. Which characteristics will you point out?
   a. sets the number of logon attempts before the account is locked out
   b. can be exceeded when a user forgets his or her password
   c. sets the length of time that an account is locked
   d. is the waiting period after the last bad logon attempt, before the reset

3. George is confused about the Account lockout duration. Which of the following will you explain to George?
   a. sets the number of logon attempts before the account is locked out
   b. can be exceeded when a user forgets his or her password
   c. sets the length of time that an account is locked
   d. uses a value of zero to indefinitely lock the account

4. Rose asks you about the Reset account threshold after provisions. Which item will you convey to Rose?
   a. sets the number of logon attempts before the account is locked out
   b. can be exceeded when a user forgets his or her password
   c. sets the length of time that an account is locked
   d. is the waiting period after the last bad logon attempt, before the reset

8

LAB 8.5 CREATE A LOCAL SECURITY GROUP POLICY

Objectives

The goal of this lab is to create a local security notification group policy. After completing this lab, you will be able to:

➤ Launch the MMC file from the desktop

➤ Set up a security policy using the Group Policy snap-in

Materials Required

This lab will require the following:

➤ Access as an administrator to a local computer running Windows 2000 Member Server

➤ Completion of Lab 8.1

Estimated completion time: **30 minutes**

ACTIVITY

1. You should still be logged on as you were at the end of Lab 8-4. If you logged out, you must log on, double-click the **UserMgt** icon on the desktop, expand **Local Computer Policy**, expand **Computer Configuration**, and then expand **Windows Settings**.

2. Expand **Local Policies**, and then click **Security Options** to view the security options in the right pane.

3. To foil unauthorized attempts to log on to your server, double-click **Do not display last user name in logon screen**, click **Enabled**, and then click **OK**.

4. Double-click **Message title for users attempting to log on**, type **Authorized Users Only** in the Local policy setting text box, and then click **OK**.

5. Double-click **Message text for users attempting to log on**, type **This is a secure system for organizational use only. All others are not permitted access** in the Local policy setting text box, and then click **OK**.

6. Click **Console**, click **Exit**, and then click **Yes** to the message prompt.

7. Log off as the administrator, press **Ctrl+Alt+Del**, view the security message, and then click **OK**.

8. Log on as **administrator**. Remain logged on for the next lab.

Certification Objectives

Objectives for Microsoft Exam 70-215: Installing, Configuring, and Administering Microsoft Windows 2000 Server:

➤ Implement, configure, manage, and troubleshoot account policy

➤ Implement, configure, manage, and troubleshoot policies in a Windows 2000 environment

Review Questions

1. Your boss asks you about measures that could be taken to protect unauthorized access to the servers in your shop. You research Windows 2000 security options. Which of the following could be implemented on your servers with the Account and Security snap-in?

   a. Blank the user account for the last logon.

   b. Turn the computer off when an illegal access occurs.

   c. Display a legal message indicating that this is a restricted computer.

   d. No legal issues are involved with unauthorized access.

LAB 8.6 REVIEWING THE SECURITY LOG FOR USER ACCOUNT CHANGES

8

Objectives

The goal of this lab is to review the user account changes audited in the previous labs. Again, auditing is the best way to track what is happening on your server. After completing this lab, you will be able to:

➤ Launch the Event Viewer

➤ Review the Security Log for account changes

Materials Required

This lab will require the following:

➤ As an administrator, access to a computer with Windows 2000 Member Server

➤ Completion of Lab 8.1, Lab 8.2, Lab 8.3, and Lab 8.4

Estimated completion time: **30 minutes**

ACTIVITY

1. Click **Start**, point to **Programs**, point to **Administrative Tools**, and then click **Event Viewer**.

2. Click the **Security Log**.

3. Review the log for logon/logoff and account management activity.

4. Double-click any entry of interest, read the information, and then click **OK**.

5. Repeat Step 4 for additional items of interest.

6. Close the **Event Viewer**.

Certification Objectives

Objectives for Microsoft Exam 70-215: Installing, Configuring, and Administering Microsoft Windows 2000 Server:

➤ Implement, configure, manage, and troubleshoot local accounts

➤ Implement, configure, manage, and troubleshoot auditing

Review Questions

1. You will train a new employee to create and update user accounts. For the next few days, you want to keep a record of the user account activity. Which items will you most likely want to audit?

    a. logon successes

    b. logon failures

    c. account management successes

    d. account management failures

CHAPTER NINE

MANAGING GROUPS, FOLDERS, FILES, AND OBJECT SECURITY

Labs included in this chapter

➤ Lab 9.1 Installing the Active Directory Users and Computers Snap-in

➤ Lab 9.2 Creating Domain Groups and Adding Domain User Accounts

➤ Lab 9.3 Creating an Audit Policy for Object Access

➤ Lab 9.4 Sharing a Folder and Assigning Permissions

➤ Lab 9.5 Testing Access to Shared Folders

Microsoft MCSE Exam #70-215 Objectives	
Objective	**Lab**
Install and configure network services for interoperability	9.1
Monitor, configure, troubleshoot, and control access to printers	9.1, 9.2, 9.3
Monitor, configure, troubleshoot, and control access to files, folders, and shared folders	9.1, 9.2, 9.4, 9.5
Monitor, configure, control, and troubleshoot access to Web sites	9.1, 9.2, 9.4, 9.5
Configure data compression	9.4, 9.5
Encrypt data on a hard disk by using Encrypting File System (EFS)	9.4, 9.5
Implement, configure, manage, and troubleshoot policies in a Windows 2000 environment	9.3
Implement, configure, manage, and troubleshoot Account Policy	9.3
Implement, configure, manage, and troubleshoot security by using the Security Configuration Tool Set	9.3

LAB 9.1 INSTALLING THE ACTIVE DIRECTORY USERS AND COMPUTERS SNAP-IN

Objectives

The goal of this lab is to install the Active Directory Users and Computers snap-in. The Active Directory tools simplify directory service administration. The Active Directory administrative tools can be used only from a computer with access to a Windows 2000 domain. Active Directory Users and Computers manages users and groups of users for your domain. With it, you can create new users and groups, add users to groups, remove users from groups, disable user and group accounts, and reset passwords for the domain.

To use the Active Directory tools remotely from a computer that is not a domain controller, you must install the Windows Active Directory Users and Computers snap-in.

After completing this lab, you will be able to:

➤ Log on to the domain with a domain account

➤ Launch the Microsoft Management Console (MMC)

➤ Add the Active Directory Users and Computers snap-in

➤ View the existing groups and users

Materials Required

This lab will require the following:

➤ Access as a domain administrator to a computer with Windows 2000 Member Server

➤ A domain name, domain administrator account, and password from your instructor

Estimated completion time: **30 minutes**

ACTIVITY

1. You should be logged on as an administrator. Press **Ctrl+Alt+Del**. Type *admin* (where *admin* is the domain administrator account supplied by your instructor), and then press **Tab**.

2. Type *password* (where *password* is the domain administrator account password supplied by your instructor).

3. Click the **Log on to** drop-down arrow, click *lonestar* (where *lonestar* is the domain name supplied by your instructor), and then click **OK** to log on.

4. Click **Start**, click **Run**, type **MMC**, and then click **OK**.

5. Click **Console**, click **Add/Remove Snap-in**, click **Add**, click the **Active Directory Users and Computers** snap-in, and then click **Add**. Click **Close**, and then click **OK**.

6. Click **Console**, click **Save As**, click the **Save in** drop-down arrow, click **Desktop**, click the **File name** text box, type **DomainMgt**, and then click **Save**.

7. Expand **Active Directory Users and Computers**, and then expand *lonestar.lonestar.com* (where *lonestar.lonestar.com* is your domain), as shown in Figure 9-1.

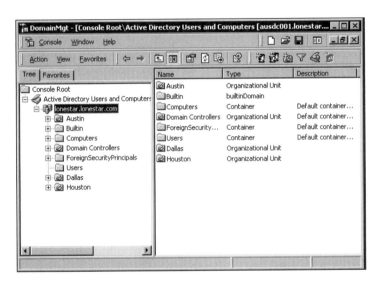

Figure 9-1   Expanded Active Directory Users and Computers

8. Click the **Users** object in the left pane to see the domain users.

9. Repeat Step 8 for additional objects in the left pane.

10. Leave the Active Directory Users and Computers open for the next lab.

Certification Objectives

Objectives for Microsoft Exam 70-215: Installing, Configuring, and Administering Microsoft Windows 2000 Server:

➤ Implement, configure, manage, and troubleshoot local accounts

➤ Monitor, configure, troubleshoot, and control access to files, folders, and shared folders

➤ Monitor, configure, troubleshoot, and control access to Web sites

➤ Install, configure, and troubleshoot shared access

Review Questions

1. Ricardo asks you about the Active Directory Users and Computers snap-in. He asks about the displayed folders. Which items will you discuss with Ricardo?

   a. The Computers folder contains the names of computers added to the domain.

   b. The Builtin folder provides the names of services deployed on the domain controller.

   c. The Domain Controllers folder contains the names of the domain controllers.

   d. The Users folder contains the user accounts for the domain.

   e. Other folders can be created to provide control over organizational units.

2. Active Directory Users and Computers is a tool that manages users and groups of users for your domain. With the Active Directory Users and Computers snap-in, which tasks can you complete? (Choose all correct answers.)

   a. create new users

   b. add users to groups

   c. remove users from groups

   d. disable user and group accounts

   e. reset passwords for the domain

LAB 9.2 CREATING DOMAIN GROUPS AND ADDING DOMAIN USER ACCOUNTS

Objectives

The goal of this lab is to set up domain local and global groups. In addition, user accounts will be added to the global group. With the Active Directory Users and Computers snap-in, you will manage domain local and global groups that control access to resources for your Windows 2000 servers. After completing this lab, you will be able to:

➤ Create a domain local group for a domain

➤ Create a global group for a domain

➤ Establish membership for a global group within a domain local group

➤ Add existing domain user accounts to a global account

Materials Required

This lab will require the following:

➤ Access as a domain administrator to a computer with Windows 2000 Server

➤ A domain administrator account and password from your instructor

➤ The names of two domain user accounts from your instructor

➤ Completion of Lab 9.1

Estimated completion time: **30 minutes**

Activity Background

Domain local security groups help you define and manage access to resources. These groups can have global groups, user accounts, or a mixture of global groups and user accounts as their members. For example, to give five users access to a particular folder, you could add all five user accounts in the folder permissions list. If, however, you later want to give the five users access to a new folder, you would again have to specify all five accounts in the permissions list for the new folder.

With a little planning, you can simplify this routine administrative task by creating a domain local group and assigning it permission to access the folder. Put the five user accounts in a global group and add this global group to the domain local group. When you want to give the five users access to a new folder, assign the group with domain local group permission to access the new folder. All members of the global group automatically receive access to the new folder.

In summary, note that security groups are used to collect users and other groups into manageable units. When assigning permissions for resources, administrators should assign those permissions to a security group rather than to individual users. The permissions are assigned once to the group, instead of several times to each individual user. Each account added to a group receives the rights and permissions defined for that group. Working with groups instead of individual users helps simplify network maintenance and administration.

ACTIVITY

1. The Active Directory Users and Computers snap-in should be open on your screen. Click *lonestar.lonestar.com* (where *lonestar.lonestar.com* is the domain).

2. Click **Action**, point to **New**, and then click **Group**.

3. To enter the Domain local Group name, type *DomainFML* (where *F* is your first initial, *M* is your middle initial, and *L* is the initial of your last name), as shown in Figure 9-2.

4. To specify the Domain local option, click the **Domain local** option button, and then click **OK**.

5. Click *lonestar.lonestar.com* (where *lonestar.lonestar.com* is the domain).

6. Click **Action**, point to **New**, and then click **Group**.

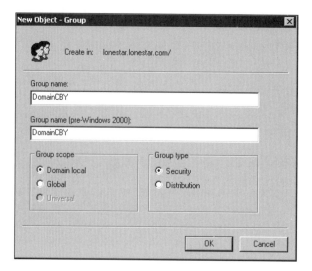

Figure 9-2   Creating a local domain group

7. To enter the Global Group name, type **GlobalFML** (where *F* is your first initial, *M* is your middle initial, and *L* is the initial of your last name), as shown in Figure 9-3.

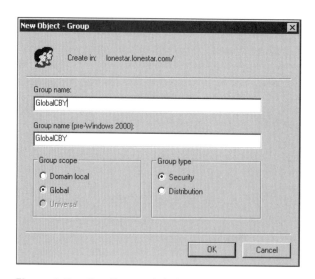

Figure 9-3   Creating a global group

8. Click **OK**.

9. To attach the Global group to the local group, double-click **GlobalFML** (where *GlobalFML* is the name of your group), click the **Member of** tab, click **Add**, click **DomainFML** (where *DomainFML* is the name of your Domain local group), click **Add**, click **OK**, click **Apply**, and then click **OK**.

10. To add users to the Global group, double-click **GlobalFML** (where *GlobalFML* is the name of your Global group), click the **Members** tab, click **Add**, double-click **User01** (where *User01* is the name of first domain user account supplied by your instructor), and then double-click **User02** (where *User02* is the name of second domain user account supplied by your instructor).

11. Click **OK**, click **Apply**, and then click **OK**.

12. Remain logged on with the domain administrator account for the next lab.

Certification Objectives

Objectives for Microsoft Exam 70-215: Installing, Configuring, and Administering Microsoft Windows 2000 Server:

➤ Implement, configure, manage, and troubleshoot local accounts

➤ Monitor, configure, troubleshoot, and control access to files, folders, and shared folders

➤ Monitor, configure, troubleshoot, and control access to Web sites

➤ Install, configure, and troubleshoot shared access

Review Questions

1. When assigning users in a domain to groups, which of the following steps should you take?
   a. Assign users to Global groups (to match screen).
   b. Assign users to Domain local groups.
   c. Add Global groups to Domain local groups.
   d. Add local groups to Global groups.

LAB 9.3 CREATING AN AUDIT POLICY FOR OBJECT ACCESS

Objectives

The goal of this lab is to install the Group Policy snap-in and use it to establish an audit policy to track access to resources in subsequent labs in this chapter. In particular, you will create a security policy to audit access to a specified file.

Before you implement resource auditing, you must turn on audit for object access. When Windows 2000 is first installed, all auditing categories are turned off. By turning on various auditing event categories, you can implement an auditing policy that suits the security needs of your organization. Audit policy is one way to locate users having trouble or deliberately trying to access prohibited areas. After completing this lab, you will be able to:

➤ Launch the Microsoft Management Console (MMC)

➤ Add the Group Policy snap-in

➤ View the domain policies

➤ Create a domain group policy to enable the auditing of object access

➤ Restart the computer to apply a domain group policy

Estimated completion time: **30 minutes**

Materials Required

This lab will require the following:

➤ Access as a domain administrator to a computer with Windows 2000 Member Server

➤ A domain name, domain administrator account, and password from your instructor

➤ Completion of Lab 9.1

ACTIVITY

1. You should be logged on to your computer with the domain administrator account. Click **Console**, click **Add/Remove Snap-in**, click **Add**, click **Group Policy**, and then click **Add**.

2. Click **Browse**, click **Default Domain Policy**, click **OK**, click **Finish**, click **Close**, and then click **OK**.

3. Click **Console**, and then click **Save**.

4. Expand **Default Domain Policy**, and then expand **Computer Configuration** to the level shown in Figure 9-4.

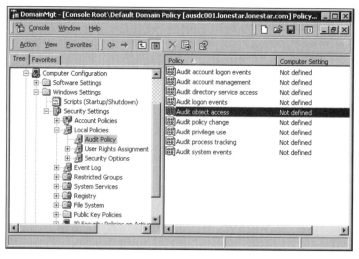

Figure 9-4   Expanded computer configuration

5. Review the Audit categories.

6. Double-click **Audit object access**.

7. Click **Define these policy settings**.

8. Click **Failure**, and then click **OK**.

9. Click **Console**, click **Exit**, and then click **Yes** to the message prompt.

10. Click **Start**, click **Shutdown**, select **Restart** from the drop-down menu, and then click **OK**.

 Restarting of the computer is required to apply the revised Domain Policy. Recall because you updated a policy for the computer configuration.

Certification Objectives

Objectives for Microsoft Exam 70-215: Installing, Configuring, and Administering Microsoft Windows 2000 Server:

➤ Implement, configure, manage, and troubleshoot local accounts

➤ Monitor, configure, troubleshoot, and control access to files, folders, and shared folders

➤ Monitor, configure, troubleshoot, and control access to Web sites

➤ Install, configure, and troubleshoot shared access

Review Questions

1. Group Policy is a tool that is required to implement auditing. Within Computer Configuration policies, to which items can you apply policies?
   a. Audit Policy
   b. Account Policies
   c. Event Log
   d. Registry
   e. File System

2. The Group Policy snap-in can be used to audit event categories. Which of the following are valid categories?
   a. account logon events
   b. object access
   c. user access
   d. policy change
   e. system

LAB 9.4 SHARING A FOLDER AND ASSIGNING PERMISSIONS

Objectives

The goal of this lab is to share a folder on a Windows 2000 member server. In the next lab, the shared folder will be accessed from a second member server. On the first member server, you will set folder share permissions and NTFS permissions. These permissions will control access to a folder. You will create a file within the shared folder and apply permissions to the file. After completing this lab, you will be able to:

➤ Create and share a folder with share permissions

➤ Set auditing for a folder

➤ Create a new text document

➤ Assign NTFS permissions to a file

Materials Required

This lab will require the following:

➤ Access as an administrator to a computer with Windows 2000 Member Server

➤ Completion of Lab 9.3

Estimated completion time: **30 minutes**

Activity Background

Share permissions set the maximum allowable actions for a shared folder. The default for share permissions is Everyone Full Control. You can leave the Everyone Full Control set in the share permissions.

With NTFS permissions, you can limit access to files and folders. The basic NTFS permissions include: Read, Write, Read & Execute, Modify, and Full Control. When multiple permissions are assigned, the resultant action is cumulative, as described below:

➤ Optionally, user is given permission to a resource.

➤ User is a member of group or groups.

➤ Group or groups are given permission to the resource.

➤ Effective permission is the cumulative permission.

➤ DENY means NO ACCESS.

➤ File permissions override directory permissions.

The cumulative share permissions and cumulative NTFS permissions are then compared and the most restrictive is the effective permission. This most restrictive permissions rule has these characteristics:

➤ User is given cumulative permission to a shared resource.

➤ User is given cumulative permission through NTFS permissions.

➤ Effective permission is the most restrictive.

In summary, it is customary to run NTFS volumes in most situations, leave share permissions set to Full Control, and use NTFS permissions to limit access.

ACTIVITY

1. Log on with the **administrator** account to a computer running Windows 2000 as a local member server.

2. Click **Start**, point to **Programs**, point to **Accessories**, and then click **Windows Explorer**.

3. Click **My Computer**, double-click **Local Disk (C:)**. (Your instructor may substitute another drive that has NTFS permissions.)

4. Right-click in the whitespace in the right pane of Windows Explorer.

5. Point to **New**, click **Folder**, and then type *ShareFML* (where *F* is your first initial, *M* is your middle initial, and *L* is the initial of your last name).

6. Right-click *ShareFML* (the folder created in Step 5) and then click **Sharing**.

7. Click **Share this folder**, but do not change the Share name, as shown in Figure 9-5.

9

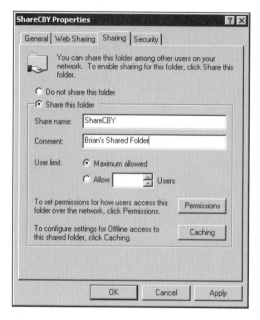

Figure 9-5   Creating a share

8. Type a comment in the **Comment** text box, and then click **Permissions**. Verify that **Everyone has Full Control** for the share permissons.

9. Click **Apply**, and then click **OK**.

10. Right-click *ShareFML*, and then click **Properties**.

11. Click the **Security** tab, and then click **Advanced**.

12. Click the **Auditing** tab, and then click **Add**.

13. Scroll through the box, locate and click **Everyone**, and then click **OK**.

14. Click **Create Files/Write Data Failed**, and then click **OK**.

15. Click **Apply**, click **OK**, click **OK**, and then click **OK**.

16. Double-click the *ShareFML* folder, and then right-click in the whitespace in the right pane.

17. Point to **New**, and then click **Text Document**.

18. Right-click **New Text Document**, and then click **Properties**.

19. Click the **Security** tab. Verify that the **Everyone** group appears, and then verify **Full Control** for the Everyone group.

20. To set NTFS permissions for the document, click **Write Deny**, and then click **Apply**.

21. Read the Security message.

22. Click **Yes**.

23. Verify that the Allow inheritable permissions from parent to propagate to this object option button is selected.

24. Click **OK**, and then close **Windows Explorer**.

Certification Objectives

Objectives for Microsoft Exam 70-215: Installing, Configuring, and Administering Microsoft Windows 2000 Server:

➤ Implement, configure, manage, and troubleshoot local accounts

➤ Monitor, configure, troubleshoot, and control access to files, folders, and shared folders

➤ Monitor, configure, troubleshoot, and control access to Web sites

➤ Install, configure, and troubleshoot shared access

Review Questions

1. Robert belongs to the Everyone, Marketing, and Accounting groups. The folder was shared with Full Control. The shared folder on a member server has the following NTFS permissions:

Groups	Permissions
Accounting	Full Control
Marketing	Deny
Everyone	Read

Robert needs access to the folder. What must you do in order for him to have Read access to this share?

a. Nothing. As a member of the Accounting group, he is given Full Control permission.

b. He has Read permission due to his membership in the Everyone group.

c. You must remove his account from the Marketing group.

d. Give his account specific permissions to access this folder.

2. A directory named \cars on an NTFS partition on your Windows 2000 server has the following NTFS permissions:

Groups	Permissions
Everyone	Deny
Engineering	Full Control
Marketing	Read Only

The folder was shared with Full Control. A file named ford.doc in this folder has Read Only access for the Engineering group. James, a member of the

Engineering group, logs on locally to the server. What permission does he have for the file ford.doc?

a. He has Deny Only access.

b. He has Read Only access.

c. He has Full Control.

d. He has Read and Write access only.

LAB 9.5 TESTING ACCESS TO A SHARED FOLDER

Objectives

The goal of this lab is to test the share and NTFS permissions for a folder on a Windows 2000 member server. On a second member server, the shared folder will be accessed from the first member server.

On the first member server, you will set folder share permissions and NTFS permissions. These permissions will control access to a folder. You will create a file within the shared folder and apply permissions to the file. You will use the Event Viewer to view the security log. These steps simulate a situation that you will likely encounter on the job. After completing this lab, you will be able to:

➤ Create and share a folder

➤ Locate and connect to a network share

➤ Test access to the shared file with NTFS Write Deny

➤ Use the Event Viewer to display the security log

Materials Required

This lab will require the following:

➤ Access as an administrator to a computer with Windows 2000 Member Server

➤ Completion of Lab 9.4

Estimated completion time: **30 minutes**

ACTIVITY

1. Move to another computer in your network that can access this computer.

2. Log on to the second computer as an **administrator**.

3. Double-click **My Network Places.**

4. Double-click **Entire Network**.

5. Click the blue text in the sentence "You may also view the entire contents of the network."

6. Double-click **Microsoft Windows Network**, and then double-click *Lonestar* (where *Lonestar* is your domain).

7. Double click *firstcomputer* (where *firstcomputer* is the computer on which you created *ShareFML*).

8. Double click *ShareFML*, and then double-click **New Text Document**.

9. Type **XXXX** in the new document that Notepad opens.

10. Click **File** on the menu bar, click **Save**, and then click the **Save** button in the dialog box.

11. Click **Yes** to the message that appears.

12. Review the resulting message. (You could not create the document because you set up a Write Deny in the previous lab.)

13. Click **OK**.

14. Click **File** on the menu bar, click **Exit**, and then click **No**.

15. **Log off** and return to the first computer.

16. Click **Start** on the desktop, point to **Programs**, point to **Administrative Tools**, and then click **Event Viewer**.

17. Click **Security Log**.

18. Double-click the first **Failure Audit**.

19. In the description, locate the object name that failed (*Hint:* C:\ShareFML\New Text Document.txt).

20. Click **OK**, and then close the **Event Viewer**.

Certification Objectives

Objectives for Microsoft Exam 70-215: Installing, Configuring, and Administering Microsoft Windows 2000 Server:

➤ Implement, configure, manage, and troubleshoot local accounts

➤ Monitor, configure, troubleshoot, and control access to files, folders, and shared folders

➤ Monitor, configure, troubleshoot, and control access to Web sites

➤ Install, configure, and troubleshoot shared access

Review Questions

1. Which program do you use to view security errors and the times that they occured?

   a. Event Viewer

   b. Security Management

   c. Disk Management

   d. Kernel Debugger

2. John asks you about the correct steps to access a shared folder. John listed the steps to access a shared folder, but he needs you to supply the correct order for the steps.

   1. Open Entire Network.
   2. Open My Network Places.
   3. Locate and click Contents.
   4. Select Microsoft Windows Network and your domain.
   5. Open the shared folder.
   6. Locate the appropriate server.

   Which of the following is the correct order of the steps?

   a. 1, 2, 3, 4, 6, 5

   b. 1, 2, 3, 4, 5, 6

   c. 2, 1, 3, 4, 6, 5

   d. 2, 1, 4, 3, 6, 5

MANAGING DFS, DISK QUOTAS, AND SOFTWARE INSTALLATION

Labs included in this chapter

➤ Lab 10.1 Creating a Distributed File System Root

➤ Lab 10.2 Adding Dfs Links to a Distributed File System Root

➤ Lab 10.3 Creating a Default Disk Quota

➤ Lab 10.4 Installing a Service Pack

➤ Lab 10.5 Viewing the Registry

Microsoft MCSE Exam #70-215 Objectives	
Objective	**Lab**
Deploy service packs	10.4
Troubleshoot failed installations	10.4
Monitor, configure, troubleshoot, and control access to files, folders, and shared folders	10.1, 10.2, 10.3
Configure hardware devices	10.5
Troubleshoot problems with hardware	10.5
Monitor and configure disk quotas	10.3

LAB 10.1 CREATING A DISTRIBUTED FILE SYSTEM ROOT

Objectives

The goal of this lab is to create a Distributed file system (Dfs) root. The Dfs topology consists of a Dfs root, one or more Dfs links, and one or more Dfs shared folders to which each Dfs link points.

A Dfs makes it easier for users to locate folders. Your users need only go to one location on the network to access files. You can spread the files and folders across multiple servers. Your users no longer need multiple drive mappings to access their files. Also, when you change the physical location of a shared folder, user access to the folder is not affected. Users can still access the folder in the same way as before because the location of the folder looks the same. After completing this lab, you will be able to:

➤ Create a shared folder

➤ Launch the Microsoft Management Console (MMC)

➤ Add the Distributed file system snap-in

➤ Create a Dfs root

Materials Required

This lab will require the following:

➤ Access to a computer running Windows 2000 Server

➤ Access to the Active Directory for lonestar.lonestar.com

➤ A domain administrator account and password to lonestar.lonestar.com

Estimated completion time: **30 minutes**

ACTIVITY

1. Log on to your computer with the **domain administrator** account and password supplied by your instructor.

2. Click **Start** on the desktop, point to **Programs**, point to **Accessories**, click **Windows Explorer**, expand **My Computer**, double-click **Local Disk (C:)**, and then right-click in the whitespace in the right pane.

3. Point to **New**, click **Folder**, and then type *DfsRootFML* (where *F* is your first initial, *M* is your middle initial, and *L* is the initial of your last name). Right-click *DfsRootFML*, click **Sharing**, and then click **Share this folder**. Do not change the share name.

4. Type a **comment** of your choosing in the Comment text box. Click **Apply**, click **OK**, and then close **Explorer**.

5. Click **Start**, click **Run**, and then type **MMC**. Click **OK**.

6. Click **Console**, click **Add/Remove Snap-in**, click **Add**, and then click **Distributed file system**. Click **Add**, click **Close**, and then click **OK**.

7. Click **Console**, click **Save As**, click the **Save in** drop-down list, and then click **Desktop**. Click the **File name** text box, type **ManDfs**, and then click **Save**.

8. Click **Distributed file system**, click **Action**, click **New Dfs Root** to start the New Dfs Root Wizard, and then click **Next**.

9. Make no further changes, and then click **Next**. Retain the lonestar.lonestar.com domain, click **Next**, retain the current name, and then click **Next**.

 If you do not see an entry for the current name, contact your instructor for help to remove an existing Dfs root.

10. Click the drop-down list to display the **share names**, click *DfsRootFML*, make no other changes, and then click **Next**.

11. Review the Dfs root name, type a **comment** of your choosing in the Comment text box, and then click **Next**.

10

12. Review the settings you chose. Click **Finish**. Leave the MMC open for the next lab, and remain logged on with the domain administrator account.

Certification Objectives

Objectives for Microsoft Exam 70-215: Installing, Configuring, and Administering Microsoft Windows 2000 Server:

➤ Monitor, configure, troubleshoot, and control access to files, folders, and shared folders

➤ Install, configure, and troubleshoot shared access

Review Questions

1. George asks you about the features of Dfs. Which of the following will you point out to George?

   a. You publish the Dfs root in the Active Directory for standalone roots.

   b. The Dfs topology consists of a Dfs root, one or more Dfs links, and one or more Dfs shared folders.

   c. You can have Dfs links point to one or more shared folders.

   d. You cannot change the physical location of the Dfs shared folders.

   e. You can spread the Dfs shared folders across multiple servers.

2. Specify the correct sequence of steps to create a Dfs root on a Windows 2000 member server with the Distributed file system snap-in.

1. Launch the MMC.
2. Create a new folder.
3. Run the Dfs Wizard.
4. Share the new folder.
5. Locate and use the existing shared new folder.
6. Type a comment describing the Dfs root.

What is the correct sequence of steps to use?
a. 1, 2, 4, 3, 5, 6
b. 1, 2, 3, 4, 5, 6
c. 2, 4, 3, 1, 5, 6
d. 2, 4, 1, 3, 5, 6

LAB 10.2 ADDING DFS LINKS TO A DISTRIBUTED FILE SYSTEM ROOT

Objectives

The objective of this lab is to add Dfs links to an existing Dfs root. You will practice adding existing shares to the Dfs root for your users. With this topology in place, your users have a central point to locate their folders and files. After completing this lab, you will be able to:

➤ Use the Distributed file system snap-in

➤ Create a Dfs link

➤ Create a Network Share to the Dfs link

➤ View the shared folders referenced by the Dfs link

Materials Required

This lab will require the following:

➤ Access to a computer with Windows 2000 Member Server

➤ Completion of Lab 10.1

➤ A computer other than your primary workstation on which to test the Dfs link

➤ The Universal Naming Convention (UNC) for two shares, which are referred to as \\server1\share1 and \\server2\share2

Estimated completion time: **30 minutes**

ACTIVITY

1. The MMC should be open and you should be logged on with the domain administrator account. Expand the **Distributed file system**, and then click **\\lonestar.lonestar.com\DfsRootFML** (where *F* is your first initial, *M* is your middle initial, and *L* is the initial of your last name).

2. Click **Action**, and then click **New Dfs link**. After completing the addition of a new Dfs link, your screen will resemble Figure 10-1.

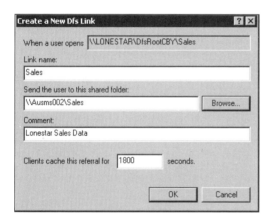

Figure 10-1   Completed Dfs link

3. Type ***share1*** (where *share1* is from the *\\server1\share1* furnished by your instructor) in the Link name text box. Type a **comment** in the Comment text box.

4. Click **Browse**, expand **Entire Network**, expand **Microsoft Windows Network**, and then expand ***server1*** (where *server1* is from the *\\server1\share1* furnished by your instructor). Your screen should resemble Figure 10-2. Click ***share1*** (where *share1* is from the *\\server1\share1* furnished by your instructor), and then click **OK**.

When the cache period elapses, the Dfs client must access the root share to update the shared folder information. Entering a lower value increases associated network traffic. A higher value reduces associated network traffic at the possible expense of accurate share information.

5. Click **\\lonestar.lonestar.com\DfsRootFML**, click **Action**, and then click **New Dfs link**.

10

Figure 10-2   Selected share

6. Type *share2* (where *share2* is from the *\\server2\share2* furnished by your instructor) in the Link name text box. Type a **comment** in the Comment text box. Click **Browse**, expand **Entire Network**, expand **Microsoft Windows Network**, and then expand *server2* (where *server2* is from the *\\server2\share2* furnished by your instructor). Click *share2* (where *share2* is from the *\\server2\share2* furnished by your instructor), click **OK**, and then click **OK**.

7. Move to a second computer. Log on to the computer using the **domain account** supplied by your instructor.

8. Right-click **Start** on the desktop, click **Explorer**, click **My Network Places**, and then double-click **Add Network Place** to start the Add Network Place Wizard.

9. Click **Browse**, and then expand *Lonestar* (where *Lonestar* is the Microsoft Windows Network name). Expand *server* (where *server* is the computer on which you built *DfsRootFML*). Click *DfsRootFML*, click **OK**, click **Next**, and then click **Finish**. You should see the folders *share1* and *share2* in the displayed window.

10. Close the window. Verify that **DfsRootFML** appears in My Network Places.

11. Close the window and log off.

12. Return to the first computer to remove the Dfs root.

13. Right-click **\\lonestar.lonestar.com\DfsRootFML**, click **Delete Dfs Root**, click **Yes**, close the **MMC**, and then click **Yes** to save the console changes.

14. To remove the Dfs root folder, right-click **Start**, click **Explorer**, expand **Local Disk (C:)**, right-click **DfsRootFML**, click **Delete**, click **Yes** to remove the folder, click **Yes** to confirm that you no longer want to share the folder, and then close the **Explorer** window.

Certification Objectives

Objectives for Microsoft Exam 70-215: Installing, Configuring, and Administering Microsoft Windows 2000 Server:

➤ Monitor, configure, troubleshoot, and control access to files, folders, and shared folders

➤ Install, configure, and troubleshoot shared access

Review Questions

1. Specify the correct sequence of steps to add a new Dfs link to an existing Dfs root on a Windows 2000 member server with the Distributed file system snap-in.

   1. Click the proper Dfs root.
   2. Launch the MMC containing the Distributed file system snap-in.
   3. Select the New Dfs link from the Action menu.
   4. Type the Dfs link name.
   5. Browse the Microsoft Windows Network for the server containing the shared folder.
   6. Select the shared folder.
   7. Click OK.

   What is the correct sequence of steps to use?
   a. 2, 1, 3, 4, 5, 6, 7
   b. 1, 2, 3, 4, 5, 6, 7
   c. 5, 6, 2, 1, 4, 3, 7
   d. 5, 6, 1, 2, 4, 3, 7

2. Brian and Lillie discuss the steps to add a Network Place. Lillie lists the steps. Brian and Lillie ask you to specify the correct sequence of steps to add a new Network Place.

   1. Launch Windows Explorer.
   2. Start the Add Network Place Wizard.
   3. Expand My Network Places.
   4. Browse for the Microsoft Windows Network.
   5. Select the desired share.
   6. Expand the desired server.
   7. Complete the instructions for the wizard.

   What is the correct sequence of steps to use?
   a. 1, 2, 3, 4, 6, 5, 7
   b. 1, 3, 2, 4, 6, 5, 7
   c. 1, 2, 4, 3, 5, 6, 7
   d. 1, 3, 2, 4, 5, 6, 7

10

LAB 10.3 CREATING A DEFAULT DISK QUOTA

Objectives

The goal of this lab is to create a default disk quota. Disk quotas track and control disk space usage for disk volumes. System administrators can configure Windows 2000 to prevent further disk space use, and to log an event when a user exceeds a specified disk space limit. If you do not want to block your users, however, you can log an event when a user exceeds a specified disk space warning level, and then periodically review the disk usage for your "high usage" users. Remember, disk space management is a major task for systems administrators. After completing this lab, you will be able to:

➤ Use Windows Explorer

➤ Establish a disk quota for a disk volume

➤ Use the Quota Entries to review existing disk usage by a user

Materials Required

This lab will require the following:

➤ Access to a computer with Windows 2000 Member Server

➤ A volume or partition on your computer that is formatted with NTFS Version 5

Estimated completion time: **30 minutes**

ACTIVITY

1. Log on with the **administrator** account.

2. Click **Start**, point to **Programs**, point to **Accessories**, click **Windows Explorer**, expand **My Computer**, and then right-click **Local Disk (C:)**.

3. Click **Properties**, click the **Quota** tab, and then check the **Enable quota management** check box, as shown in Figure 10-3.

4. Verify that the Deny disk space to users exceeding quota limit check box is cleared. If it is not cleared, click it to clear the check mark.

You can configure disk quotas to deny disk space to users of a volume who exceed their assigned quota limits. When they reach their quota limits, users must delete existing files from the volume prior to storing additional files. The response to a user exceeding the quota limit depends on each individual program. To the program itself, however, it will appear that the volume is full.

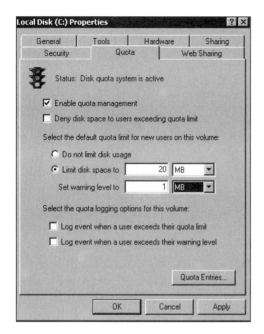

Figure 10-3   Configuring disk quotas

5. Click the **Limit disk space to** option button, type **20** in the Limit disk space to text box, and then select **MB** from the Limit disk space to drop-down list. Type **1** in the Set warning level to text box, and then select **MB** from the Set warning level to drop-down list.

You can specify that users can exceed their quota limits. Enabling quotas and not limiting disk space use are useful when you want to track disk space use on a per-user basis. You can specify that the system log an event when your users exceed their quota limits.

6. Click **Apply** and then click **OK** to scan the drive and to enable the quotas.

7. Click **Quota Entries** and then review the Status Entries. You should see one or more entries for user accounts exceeding the enabled quotas. Close the Quota Entries window.

8. Click the **Help** button, and then click the **Stop** icon. Read the displayed text.

9. Click the **Help** button, and then click an additional item of interest. Read the displayed text.

10. Repeat Step 9 for additional items.

11. Click **OK**, and then close **Explorer**.

Certification Objectives

Objectives for Microsoft Exam 70-215: Installing, Configuring, and Administering Microsoft Windows 2000 Server:

➤ Monitor and configure disk quotas

➤ Monitor, configure, troubleshoot, and control access to files, folders, and shared folders

➤ Install, configure, and troubleshoot shared access

Review Questions

1. Brian and Lillie discuss setting up disk quotas. They ask you to clarify the options that are available in the disk quota system. Which of the following will you point out to Brian and Lillie?

   a. Disk quotas are set for each individual volume.

   b. Disk quotas can be toggled on or off for the volume.

   c. Users can be denied additional disk space when their quotas are exceeded.

   d. Volume disk quotas override individual disk quotas.

   e. With the proper settings, programs can detect that no space exists on the volume when quota is exceeded.

   f. Users will receive warning messages when they exceed the warning level.

   g. Default limits are set for new users of the volume.

2. George is setting up disk quotas on the new server that will be installed on the tenth floor. He asks you to review his plan. He established the following goals for disk space management:

   1. Deny disk space to users exceeding 35 MB.
   2. Warn users when 5 MB of free space remains.
   3. Log users exceeding their quota limits.
   4. Log users exceeding their warning limits.

   George will complete the following installation steps:

   1. Format volume C: with FAT for the Windows 2000 operating system files.
   2. Format volume D: with NTFS for the user data files.
   3. Deny disk space to users exceeding their quotas.
   4. Limit disk space to 35 MB.
   5. Set the warning level to 5 MB.
   6. Set logging for users exceeding their quota limits.
   7. Set logging for users exceeding their warning limits.

What will you tell George about his plan?

a. Goal 1 is met.

b. Goal 2 is met.

c. Goal 3 is met.

d. Goal 4 is met.

e. He overlooked an option; no goals will be met.

LAB 10.4 INSTALLING A SERVICE PACK

Objectives

The objective of this lab is to install a service pack. The service pack is a collection of updates that fixes issues in the Windows 2000 operating system. As a network administrator, you will be required to install service packs on your servers. You can use a server to redistribute a service pack. When you do so, you will connect to a shared folder that contains the service pack. From the network share, you will execute the program to install the service pack. After completing this lab, you will be able to:

➤ Use Windows Explorer to locate the service pack

➤ Attach to a existing network share

➤ Execute the service pack update program

➤ Uninstall the service pack

Materials Required

This lab will require the following:

➤ Access to a computer that is running Windows 2000 Member Server and requires a service pack

➤ The UNC for the share to \\SPserver\sp1 where the service pack is located

Estimated completion time: **60 minutes**

ACTIVITY

1. Log on to the computer with an **administrator** account.

For the service pack install to complete successfully, it is recommended that you close any running applications at this time.

2. Right-click **Start**, and then click **Explorer**.

3. Click **My Network Places**, double-click **Entire Network**, and then click **entire contents** to browse the network.

4. Double-click the **Microsoft Windows Network** icon, and then double-click *lonestar* (where *lonestar* is the Microsoft Windows Network name).

5. Double-click *Spserver* (where *Spserver* is the server with the files service pack).

6. Double-click *Sp1* (where *Sp1* is the share with the files service pack).

7. Double-click the **i386** folder, and then double-click the **Update** folder.

8. Double-click the **Update program** icon to start the service pack update.

9. Scroll to read the license agreement. Click **Accept the license agreement**.

10. Retain the Backup files necessary to uninstall option.

11. Click **Readme**, read the section on installing the service pack, and then close the **Internet Explorer** window.

12. Click **Install**. Watch the progress bar.

 Depending on processor speed, available memory, and network traffic, Step 12 could take 15–20 minutes.

13. Click **Restart** to restart the computer.

14. If your instructor asks you to leave the service pack installed, **STOP** at this step. If not, continue with Step 15.

15. Log on to the computer with the **administrator** account.

16. Click **Start**, point to **Settings**, click **Control Panel**, and then double-click **Add/Remove Programs**.

17. Click **Change or Remove Programs**. Locate and click the **Windows 2000 service pack**, and then click **Change/Remove**.

18. Read the Windows 2000 service pack uninstall message, and then click **Yes**.

19. Watch the progress bar as the backup files are copied.

20. Click **Restart** to restart the computer.

Certification Objectives

Objectives for Microsoft Exam 70-215: Installing, Configuring, and Administering Microsoft Windows 2000 Server:

➤ Display a service pack

Review Questions

1. You are preparing an action plan to install the new service pack for your Windows 2000 servers. Which items will you include in your action plan?

    a. Create a list of servers requiring the installation of a service pack.

    b. Copy the service pack to a member server.

    c. Schedule a time for the installation of the service pack on each server.

    d. Read the documentation received with the service pack.

    e. Test the installation of the service pack on a non-production server.

LAB 10.5 VIEWING THE REGISTRY

Objectives

The goal of this lab is to view the Registry. System configuration information is centrally located in the Registry. Because one incorrect edit to the Registry can disable the operating system, Microsoft recommends that you make a backup copy of the Registry before making changes to it. After completing this lab, you will be able to:

➤ Launch the REGEDT32 Registry Editor

➤ Expand Registry keys in the tree pane

➤ View data in the data pane

➤ Explore the relationship between the Registry and the Control Panel Mouse applet

Materials Required

This lab will require the following:

➤ Access to a computer running Windows 2000 Member Server

Estimated completion time: **30 minutes**

ACTIVITY

1. Log on with the **administrator** account. Close any windows left open from the previous lab.

There are two Registry Editors available with Windows 2000 Server. Regedit is easier to use when searching for keys and data in the Registry. Regedt32 is the preferred editor for registry management.

2. Click **Start**, click **Run**, and then type **regedt32** (there is no "i" in regedt32).

After you open the Run dialog box in Step 2, you could complete the task by selecting regedt32 from the Open drop-down list, if regedt32 ran before.

3. Click **OK**.

4. Click **Window** on the menu bar, and then click **HKEY_CURRENT_USER on Local Machine**.

5. Click **View** on the menu bar, and then click **Tree and Data**.

6. Expand **Control Panel**, and then locate and click **Mouse**.

7. View the mouse settings in the right pane, as shown in Figure 10-4. In particular, note DoubleClickSpeed.

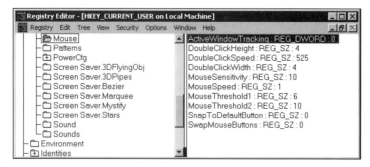

Figure 10-4   Mouse registry settings

 Changing these values for the mouse may make it difficult to use your mouse!

8. If the Registry Editor is in full screen, click the window's **Restore** button.

9. Size the **Registry** window to fit the bottom-half of your display.

10. Click **View** on the menu bar, and then click **Data Only**.

11. Click **Start** on the desktop, point to **Settings**, click **Control Panel**, and then double-click **Mouse**.

12. Move the **Mouse Properties** window until the Registry window is visible.

13. Locate the **DoubleClickSpeed** and then record the value on a piece of paper.

14. Return to the **Mouse Properties** window. Click the **Buttons** tab, and then drag the **Double-click speed** slider to a slower setting.

15. Double-click in the **Test** area.

16. Drag the **Double-click speed** slider to another setting.

17. Repeat Steps 15 and 16 until you are pleased with the responsiveness of the mouse.

18. Click **Apply**.

19. Return to the **Registry Editor** window. Locate the **DoubleClickSpeed** and compare it to the value recorded in Step 13.

20. Repeat Steps 13 through 19 for different mouse speeds.

21. Return to the **Mouse Properties** window, and then click **Cancel**.

22. Return to the **Registry Editor** window.

23. Click **View** on the menu bar, and then click **Tree and Data**.

24. Click **Window** on the menu bar, and then click **HKEY_LOCAL_MACHINE on Local Machine**.

25. Expand **Software**, expand **Microsoft**, scroll and locate **Windows NT**, and then expand **Windows NT**. Expand **CurrentVersion**.

26. Locate and view the CurrentVersion. Locate and view the **ProductName** (If you do not see CurrentVersion or ProductName, ask your instructor for assistance.)

27. Close the **Registry Editor** window and then close the **Control Panel**.

Certification Objectives

Objectives for Microsoft Exam 70-215: Installing, Configuring, and Administering Microsoft Windows 2000 Server:

➤ Configure hardware devices

➤ Troubleshoot problems with hardware

Review Questions

1. You try to recall where local computer software configuration information is kept in the Registry. Which key has software configuration information for all users of your server?
   a. HKEY_MACHINE
   b. HKEY_USERS
   c. HKEY_CURRENT_USER
   d. HKEY_CLASSES_ROOT
   e. HKEY_LOCAL_MACHINE

2. You are troubleshooting and know that there is a bad value in the Registry, but you do not know where. Which of the following tools can speed the search process?
   a. Windows 3*x* Regedit
   b. Windows 9x version of Registry Editor, REGEDIT
   c. Windows 2000 version of Registry Editor, REGEDT32
   d. Windows regpad

INSTALLING AND MANAGING PRINTERS

<table>
<tr><td colspan="2" align="center">Labs included in this chapter</td></tr>
<tr><td>➤ Lab 11.1 Creating a Network Printer</td></tr>
<tr><td>➤ Lab 11.2 Controlling Print Jobs</td></tr>
<tr><td>➤ Lab 11.3 Configuring the Print Server Properties</td></tr>
<tr><td>➤ Lab 11.4 Creating Multiple Printers</td></tr>
<tr><td>➤ Lab 11.5 Creating a Printer Pool</td></tr>
</table>

Microsoft MCSE Exam #70-215 Objectives	
Objective	**Lab**
Install and configure network services for interoperability	11.1, 11.2, 11.3
Monitor, configure, troubleshoot, and control access to printers	11.1, 11.2, 11.3, 11.4, 11.5
Configure hardware devices	11.1, 11.3
Update device drivers	11.1
Troubleshoot problems with hardware	11.1, 11.3

LAB 11.1 CREATING A NETWORK PRINTER

Objectives

The goal of this lab is to create a printer. Recall that Microsoft refers to the print driver software as the printer and to the printer hardware as a printing device. Network administrators attach printing devices on servers to provide printers for their users. After completing this lab exercise, you will be able to:

➤ Launch the Add Printer Wizard

➤ Configure the printer for an attached printing device

➤ Share a printer for network access

➤ Test the printer connection

Materials Required

This lab will require the following:

➤ Administrative access to a computer running Windows 2000 Member Server

➤ A printer, if you want to be able to print a test page

Estimated completion time: **30 minutes**

ACTIVITY

1. Log on to the server with a local **administrator** account. Click **Start**, point to **Settings**, and then click **Printers**.

You will be unable to add a printer if a printer already exists on the system. To remove a printer, right-click the appropriate printer icon, click Delete, and then click Yes to confirm the deletion. If this is the last or default printer, click OK to the message on your screen.

2. Double-click **Add Printer** to start the Add Printer Wizard. Click **Next**, clear the **Automatically detect and install** check box, and then click **Next**.

3. Click the **port number** for the attached printer (for most computers, this will be LPT1). Click **Next**.

4. Scroll to locate the manufacturer of the printer, as shown in Figure 11-1. To quickly jump to the manufacturer, you can also press the first letter of the manufacturer's name. For example, you could press **H** for Hewlett Packard.

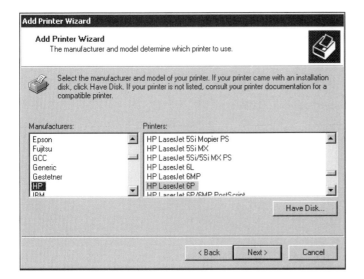

Figure 11-1   Selecting a printer

5. Press **Tab**, and then scroll and locate the printer.

Have Disk is used to install a specialized printer driver or a printer that is not on the Windows 2000 CD-ROM. You should click the Have Disk only if you have the disk for a new printer driver.

6. Click **Next**. (If there is an existing printer installed, leave the Keep existing driver (recommended) check box selected, and then click **Next**.)

7. Type **serverpr01** (where *server* is the name of the server and *pr01* indicates the first printer).

8. Click **Next**. Click **Share as**, type **serverpr01** for the share name (where *server* is the name of the server and *pr01* indicates the first printer), and then click **Next**.

If you share a printer with MS-DOS computers, do not use more than eight characters for the printer's share name. You can lengthen the name by adding a period followed by no more than three characters, but you cannot use spaces in the name. If the share name you are using is more than 12 characters, click Yes to keep the share name.

9. Type a **location** that will identify where to find the printer, as shown in Figure 11-2, and then press **Tab**.

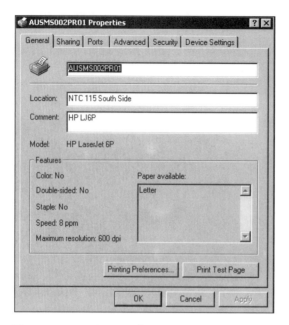

Figure 11-2   Setting descriptive text

10. Type a **comment** that will indicate the capabilities of the printer, and then click **Next**.

Location and printer capability information will assist your users when they attempt to locate a printer with the capabilities that they require for print output.

11. Click **Yes** to the Do you want to print a test page? prompt. However, if the printer is not physically attached to the server, click **No** to bypass the test page. This will avoid possible error conditions. Click **Next**.

12. Review the **printer settings**, click **Finish**, and then review the test page. If the output is readable, click **OK**.

You may want to use the Troubleshooter to resolve a printer setup problem. Clicking Troubleshooter will walk you through a series of troubleshooting steps.

13. Remain logged on with the Printers folder open for the next lab.

Certification Objectives

Objectives for Microsoft Exam 70-215: Installing, Configuring, and Administering Microsoft Windows 2000 Server:

➤ Configure hardware devices

➤ Troubleshoot problems with hardware

➤ Install and configure network services for interoperability

➤ Monitor, configure, troubleshoot, and control access to printers

➤ Install, configure, and troubleshoot shared access

Review Questions

1. Brian and Lillie discuss setting up network printers with the Add Printer Wizard. They ask you about the correct sequence of the following steps:

   1. Locate the manufacturer and printer.
   2. Name the printer.
   3. Open the Printers folder.
   4. Start the Add Printer Wizard.
   5. Select the port for the printer.
   6. Share the printer.
   7. Review the printer settings.
   8. Review the printer test page.

   Which of the following will you indicate as the correct sequence of steps?

   a. 4, 5, 6, 7, 8

   b. 3, 4, 5, 6, 7, 8

   c. 3, 4, 5, 1, 2, 6, 7, 8

   d. 3, 4, 1, 2, 5, 6, 7, 8

2. You are installing a new printer for your Windows 2000 users. You are using the Add Printer Wizard. You locate the manufacturer in the Add Printer Wizard dialog box. However, you are unable to locate the printer description. Which of the following would be acceptable options to install the printer driver for your new printer?

   a. Use the Windows 98 driver provided by the manufacturer.

   b. Download the new Windows 2000 driver from the Microsoft Web site.

   c. Download the new Windows 2000 driver from the manufacturer's Web site.

   d. Use the printer driver for the previous model.

11

LAB 11.2 CONTROLLING PRINT JOBS

Objectives

The goal of this lab is to control print jobs. As a network administrator, you will help your users with network printing. From the Printer dialog box, you can control jobs for a printer. After completing this lab, you will be able to:

➤ Open the Printer dialog box

➤ Pause the printer queue

➤ Print a document

➤ Cancel a document in the print queue

➤ Cancel all the jobs in the queue

Materials Required

This lab will require the following:

➤ Access to a computer running Windows 2000 Member Server

➤ Completion of Lab 11.1

Estimated completion time: **30 minutes**

ACTIVITY

1. You should be logged on with the Printers folder open. Double-click ***serverpr01*** (where *server* is the name of the server and *pr01* indicates the first printer) to open the Printer dialog box.

2. Click the **Printer** menu, and then click **Pause Printing**.

The printer output must be paused. This will permit the simulation of the control of job output without wasting paper (and precious trees!).

3. Click **Start**, point to **Programs**, point to **Accessories**, click **Wordpad**, and then type any brief message. Click the **Print** button, and then minimize **Wordpad**.

4. Return to the **Printer dialog box** and review the print job status. Click **Document** in the Printer dialog box, click the **Document** menu, and observe the document options.

5. Click the **Printer** menu and observe the printer options.

6. Right-click the **Document** in the dialog box, and then click **Cancel** to remove the print job.

7. Return to **Wordpad**. Press the **Print** button three times, close **Wordpad**, but do not save changes to the document.

8. Return to the **Printer dialog box** and review the print job status. Click the **Printer** menu, click **Cancel all documents**, and then click **Yes**. Click the **Printer** menu, click **Pause Printing** to re-enable printing, and then close the **Printer dialog box**.

 Pause Printing is a toggle menu selection. When the menu entry has a check, the output is paused. Clicking Pause Printing a second time will clear the check mark and re-enable the printer.

9. Leave the Printers folder open and remain logged on for the next lab.

Certification Objectives

Objectives for Microsoft Exam 70-215: Installing, Configuring, and Administering Microsoft Windows 2000 Server:

➤ Install and configure network services for interoperability

➤ Monitor, configure, troubleshoot, and control access to printers

➤ Install, configure, and troubleshoot shared access

Review Questions

1. A peer asks you about controlling printers with the Printer dialog box. He is confused about pausing, resuming, and restarting documents. Which of the following will you point out in your discussion? (Choose all correct answers.)

    a. When you restart a document, it starts printing again from the beginning.

    b. When you restart a document, it starts printing again from the page that was last printed.

    c. Once a document starts printing, it will finish printing even if you pause it.

    d. If you pause a document, it will not print until you resume printing.

    e. If you resume printing, the document will continue printing unless higher priority documents are waiting to print.

LAB 11.3 CONFIGURING THE PRINT SERVER PROPERTIES

Objectives

The goal of this lab is to review the print server properties for a printer. After completing this lab, you will be able to:

➤ Open the Print Properties dialog box

➤ Review the Tabbed Print Properties dialog box entries

➤ Review the Advanced Print Properties dialog box entries

Materials Required

This lab will require the following:

➤ Access to a computer running Windows 2000 Member Server

➤ Completion of Labs 11.1 and 11.2

Estimated completion time: **30 minutes**

ACTIVITY

1. You should have the Printers folder open and be logged on.

   Right-click **serverpr01** (where *server* is the name of the server and *pr01* indicates the first printer). Click **Printing Preferences**, and then review the preferences for the printer. Click **OK**.

2. Right-click **serverpr01** (where *server* is the name of the server and *pr01* indicates the first printer). Click **Properties**.

3. Click the **Sharing** tab and review the **Shared as** shared name.

To provide drivers for other operating systems, click the Additional Drivers button, click the additional operating systems check box, click OK, and then follow the instructions for the selected operating system.

4. Click the **Ports** tab and verify the port used for this printer.

5. Click the **Advanced** tab and review its contents.

6. Click the **Security** tab, click **Everyone**, and then verify that **Print Allow** is set.

7. Click the **Device Settings** tab and review its contents.

8. Click the **Advanced** tab.

9. Click the **Help** button, click the **Spool print documents so program finishes printing faster** option button, and then read the explanation.

10. Click the **Help** button, click the **Start printing after last page is spooled** option button, and then read the explanation.

11. Click the **Help** button. Click the **Start printing immediately** option text. Read the explanation.

12. Click the **Help** button. Click the **Print directly to the printer** option text. Read the explanation.

13. Click the **Help** button. Click the **Hold mismatched documents** check box. Read the explanation.

14. Click the **Help** button. Click the **Print spooled documents first** check box. Read the explanation.

15. Click the **Help** button. Click the **Keep printed documents** check box. Read the explanation.

16. Click the **Help** button, click the **Enable advanced printing features** check box, and then read the explanation.

17. Click the **Print Processor** button, and then read the text at the top of the Print Processor dialog box.

18. Review the default data type information, click **Cancel**, and then click **Cancel**.

19. Leave the Printers folder open and remain logged on for the next lab.

Certification Objectives

Objectives for Microsoft Exam 70-215: Installing, Configuring, and Administering Microsoft Windows 2000 Server:

➤ Configure hardware devices

➤ Troubleshoot problems with hardware

➤ Install and configure network services for interoperability

➤ Monitor, configure, troubleshoot, and control access to printers

➤ Install, configure, and troubleshoot shared access

Review Questions

1. You are concerned about the printer being used by the Graphics department at your company. Their graphics programs require a considerable amount of time to render the pages prior to printing. They complain that the printers often print only parts of drawings. Which printer settings could alleviate problems with their network printer?

   a. Spool print documents

   b. Start printing after last page is spooled

     c. Start printing immediately

     d. Print directly to the printer

     e. Print spooled documents first

     f. Keep printed documents

2. You plan to implement a new setup requirement for printers installed by your department. You establish the following goals for the setup requirements:

    1. Specify uniform naming conventions for printers
    2. Allow users to return to their applications without waiting for printers
    3. Provide priority to spooled documents
    4. Check the printer setup and match it to the document

    You establish a printer naming scheme that includes the server name and the printer name. You select the following options on the Advanced printer tab: Spool print documents; Start printing after last page is spooled, and Print spooled documents first. You ask a peer to review your plan. Which goals will your peer indicate as met?

     a. Goal 1 is met.

     b. Goal 2 is met.

     c. Goal 3 is met.

     d. Goal 4 is met.

     e. No goals are met.

LAB 11.4 CREATING MULTIPLE PRINTERS

Objectives

The goal of this lab is to create multiple printers. By creating multiple printers, network administrators can tailor the printing software for special conditions. Each software printer will print to the same printer device.

As a network administrator, you can use the Priority and Availability options to set up printers for special situations. In this lab, you will set up a high-priority printer (*serverpr01M*) for use by the managers in the department. For overnight, high-volume printing, you will set up the *serverpr01N* printer. After completing this lab, you will be able to:

    ➤ Launch the Add Printer Wizard

    ➤ Establish a printer schedule

    ➤ Establish a priority for a printer

    ➤ Control access to a printer

Materials Required

This lab will require the following:

> Access to a computer running Windows 2000 Member Server

> Completion of Labs 11.1, 11.2, and 11.3

> Two domain local group names from your instructor to control access to the printers

Estimated completion time: **30 minutes**

ACTIVITY

1. You should have the Printers folder open and be logged on. Click the **View** menu, click **Small Icons**, and then double-click **Add Printer** to start the Add Printer Wizard. Click **Next**.

2. Retain the local printer, clear the **Automatically detect and install** check box, and then click **Next**.

3. Retain the **Use the following port** option button, click the **port number** for the attached printer (for most computers, this will be LPT1), and then click **Next**.

4. Scroll to locate the manufacturer of the printer.

5. Press **Tab**, and then scroll to locate the printer.

6. Click **Next**. (If you are the second or successive person to install this driver, retain the **Keep existing driver (recommended)** option button, and then click **Next**.)

7. Type *serverpr01M* (where *server* is the name of the server and *pr01* indicates the first printer).

8. Click **Next**, click **Share as**, type *serverpr01M* for the share name (where *server* is the name of the server and *pr01* indicates the first printer), and then click **Next**. (If the Share name that you entered...message appears, click **Yes**.)

9. Type a **location** that will identify where to find the printer, and then press **Tab**.

10. Type a **comment** that will indicate this printer is to be used for managers within the department, and then click **Next**.

11. Click **No** to the Do you want to print a test page? message.

12. Click **Next**, review the **printer settings**, and then click **Finish**.

13. Return to the **Printers folder**.

14. Right-click *serverpr01M*, click **Properties**, and then click the **Advanced** tab.

15. Change the Priority to **25**, as shown in Figure 11-3, and then click **Apply**.

11

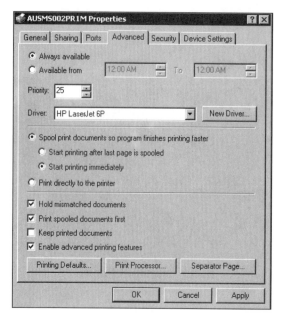

Figure 11-3   Setting printer priority

16. Click the **Security** tab, and then click **Add**.

17. Examine Figure 11-4, click *GLManagers*, click **Add**, click **OK**, click **Apply**, and then click **OK**.

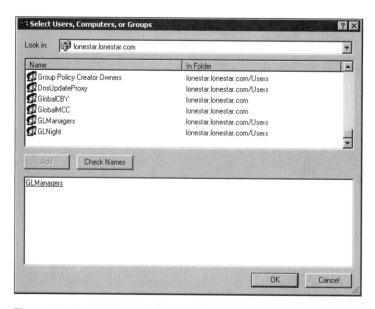

Figure 11-4   Setting printer permissions

18. Repeat Steps 1 through 13 for *serverpr01N* using the next available port.

19. Right-click *serverpr01N*, click **Properties**, and then click the **Advanced** tab.

20. Make the printer available from **6:00PM** to **7:00AM**.

21. Change Priority to **1**, and then click **Apply**.

22. Click the **Security** tab, and then click **Add**.

23. Locate and click *GLManagers*, and then click **Add**. Locate and click *GLNight*. Click **Add**, click **OK**, click **Apply**, and then click **OK**.

24. Leave the Printers folder open and remain logged on for the next lab.

Certification Objectives

Objectives for Microsoft Exam 70-215: Installing, Configuring, and Administering Microsoft Windows 2000 Server:

➤ Install and configure network services for interoperability

➤ Monitor, configure, troubleshoot, and control access to printers

➤ Install, configure, and troubleshoot shared access

Review Questions

1. You are consulting for a small firm. The managers ask you to set up an expedite printer for small, fast jobs. You are taking an Install 2000 Server class at a local college. You recall that you can control the printer queue. You decide to save the company some money. Which of the following choices will meet the managers' requirements?

   a. Configure a printer, assign permissions to the Managers group, and set the priority to 1.

   b. Configure a printer, assign permissions to the Managers group, and set the priority to 49.

   c. Configure a printer, assign permissions to the Managers group, and start printing immediately.

   d. Configure a printer, assign permissions to the Managers group, and print directly to the print device.

11

LAB 11.5 CREATING A PRINTER POOL

Objectives

The goal of this lab is to create a printer pool. Remember that Microsoft refers to the software as a printer and the hardware as a printing device. Network administrators attach multiple printing devices to provide printer pools for their users. After completing this lab, you will be able to:

➤ Launch the Add Printer Wizard

➤ Configure the printer for an attached printing device

➤ Share a printer for network access

➤ Test the printer connection

Materials Required

This lab will require the following:

➤ Access to a computer running Windows 2000 Member Server

Estimated completion time: **30 minutes**

ACTIVITY

1. You should have the Printers folder open and be logged on. Double-click **Add Printer** to start the Add Printer Wizard. Click **Next**.

2. Clear the **Automatically detect and install** check box, and then click **Next**.

3. Click **LPT2**, and then click **Next**.

4. Scroll to locate the manufacturer of the printer.

5. Press **Tab**, and then scroll and select the printer.

6. Click **Next**, and then click **Next**.

7. Type *serverpr02* (where *server* is the name of the server and *pr02* indicates the second printer).

8. Click **Next**, click the **Do not share this printer** option button, and then click **Next**.

9. Click **No** to the message box, and then click **Next**.

10. Review the **printer settings**, and then click **Finish**.

11. Repeat Steps 1 through 10 using *serverpr03* and *lpt3*.

12. Right-click *serverpr01*, click **Properties**, and then click the **Ports** tab, as shown in Figure 11-5.

13. Click the **Enable printer pooling** check box.

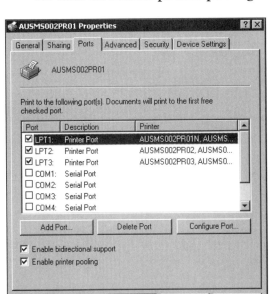

Figure 11-5   Creating a printer pool

14. Click the **LPT2** and **LPT3** check boxes.

15. Click **Apply**, and then click **OK**.

Certification Objectives

Objectives for Microsoft Exam 70-215: Installing, Configuring, and Administering Microsoft Windows 2000 Server:

➤ Configure hardware devices

➤ Troubleshoot problems with hardware

➤ Install and configure network services for interoperability

➤ Monitor, configure, troubleshoot, and control access to printers

➤ Install, configure, and troubleshoot shared access

Review Questions

1. You consider setting up a printer pool. Which conditions should be met for the efficient operation of a printer pool?
   a. All print devices must be connected to the same printer.
   b. All print devices must use the same print driver.
   c. All print devices must use the same printer port.
   d. All print devices should be located close to each other.
   e. All print devices must be controlled by the same server.

REMOTE ACCESS AND VIRTUAL PRIVATE NETWORKS

Labs included in this chapter

➤ Lab 12.1 Install Remote Access Service

➤ Lab 12.2 Configuring a User Account with RAS Options

➤ Lab 12.3 Test access to Remote Access Server

➤ Lab 12.4 Test access to a Virtual Private Network Server

➤ Lab 12.5 Review Connections to a Remote Access Server

Microsoft MCSE Exam #70-215 Objectives

Objective	Lab
Configure hardware devices	12.1
Troubleshoot problems with hardware	12.1
Install, configure, and troubleshoot shared access	12.2, 12.5
Install, configure, and troubleshoot a virtual private network (VPN)	12.1, 12.2, 12.3, 12.4, 12.5
Install, configure, and troubleshoot network protocols	12.1, 12.4
Install and configure network services	12.1
Configure, monitor, and troubleshoot remote access	12.1, 12.2, 12.3, 12.4, 12.5
Configure the properties of a connection	12.1, 12.3, 12.4, 12.5
Install, configure, and troubleshoot network adapters and drivers	12.1
Implement, configure, manage, and troubleshoot local accounts	12.2

Lab 12.1 Install Remote Access Service

Objectives

The goal of this lab is to install Remote Access Service (RAS). RAS is part of the integrated Routing and Remote Access Service (RRAS). Installing a RAS server enables a VPN server.

With RAS, you can permit remote or mobile workers access to your network. When your users run RAS software and initiate a connection to the RAS server, the RAS server authenticates users and services sessions until they are terminated by the user or network administrator. All services typically available to a LAN-connected user (including file and print sharing, Web server access, and messaging) are enabled by the RAS connection. After completing this lab, you will be able to:

> ➤ Set up a modem for RAS

> ➤ Launch the RRAS

> ➤ Run the RRAS Setup Wizard

> ➤ Set up the DHCP Relay Agent to forward DHCP requests

> ➤ Review the RAS and Virtual Private Network (VPN) ports

> ➤ Set up authentication options, such as MS CHAP V2 and MS CHAP

Materials Required

This lab will require the following:

> ➤ Access to a Windows 2000 member server. (Your instructor added the server to the RAS and IAS Servers group in Active Directory.)

> ➤ The IP address of a DHCP server

> ➤ A modem and a modem line. (If necessary, a telco line simulator can facilitate the modem line and PBX, or you can use a null modem cable.)

Estimated completion time: **30 minutes**

Activity

1. Log on to the member server with the **administrator** account.

2. Click **Start**, point to **Settings**, click **Control Panel**, and then double-click **Phone and Modem Options**.

If the modem is installed, click the modem entry, and then click Remove.

3. Type your **area code** into the What area code (or city code) are you in now? text box, and then click **OK**.

If a previous student set up a modem through this server, the area code option does not appear.

4. Click the **Modems** tab, click **Add**, click **Don't detect my modem; I will select it from a list**, and then click **Next**. Locate and select both the **manu-facturer** and the **model**, and then click **Next**. Click your **communications port**, click **Next**, click **Finish**, and then click **OK**.

5. Click **Start**, point to **Programs**, point to **Administrative Tools**, and then click **Routing and Remote Access**.

If Routing and Remote Access is enabled (this is indicated by a green up arrow on the server), click the server name, click Action, and then click Disable Routing and Remote Access.

6. Click the **server name**, click **Action**, click **Configure and Enable Routing and Remote Access** to start the Routing and Remote Access Server Setup Wizard, and then click **Next**.

7. Click **Remote Access Server**, click **Next**, and then click **Next** to select TCP/IP as your protocol.

8. Do not change the **Automatically** option button. Click **Next**, click **OK** to any message that appears, click **Next**, and then click **Finish**.

9. Click **OK** to any message boxes that might appear.

10. Expand the **server**, and then expand **IP Routing**. Right-click **DHCP Relay Agent**, click **Properties**, type the **IP address** of the DHCP server provided by your instructor, click **Add**, click **Apply**, and then click **OK**.

11. Double-click **Ports**. Review the right pane. It should resemble Figure 12-1.

12 Right-click **Ports** in the left pane, click **Properties**, click **Configure**, verify that the **Remote access connections** (inbound only) check box is checked, click **OK,** click **Apply**, and then click **OK**.

13. Right-click your **server**, click **Properties**, click the **Security** tab, click the **Authentication Methods** button, and then check **MS-CHAP** and **MS-CHAP v2**, if necessary.

14. Click **OK**, click **Apply**, and then click **OK**.

15. Close the **Routing and Remote Access** dialog box. Log off the computer. Remain at the same computer for the next lab.

12

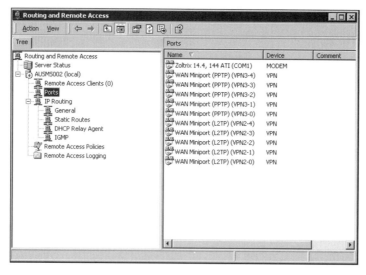

Figure 12-1 RAS and VPN ports

Certification Objectives

Objectives for Microsoft Exam 70-215: Installing, Configuring, and Administering Microsoft Windows 2000 Server:

➤ Configure hardware devices

➤ Install, configure, and troubleshoot a virtual private network

➤ Configure, monitor, and troubleshoot Remote Access

➤ Install, configure, and troubleshoot network protocols

Review Questions

1. George asks you about the features of a RAS server. Which of the following will you point out to George?

   a. It permits mobile office workers to dial in to your network.

   b. It permits access to e-mail and Web servers.

   c. It permits applications to be launched over the dial-in connection.

   d. The RAS server checks the login IDs and passwords.

   e. The network administrator cannot terminate a connection.

2. Specify the correct sequence of steps to install a modem on a Windows 2000 member server.

   1. Type the area code and outside line code.
   2. Select the Modems tab.
   3. Select the option to skip PNP.

4. Locate and select the manufacturer of the modem.
5. Locate and select the model of the modem.
6. Select a communications port.
7. Launch the Phone and Modem Options applet in the Control Panel.
8. Finish the wizard dialog.
   a. 7, 2, 3, 4, 5, 7, 8
   b. 7, 1, 2, 4, 5, 6, 8
   c. 7, 2, 3, 4, 5, 6, 8
   d. 7, 1, 2, 3, 4, 5, 6, 8

3. Which of the following can you configure with Routing and Remote Access Server Setup Wizard.
   a. DHCP relay agent
   b. RAS
   c. VPN server
   d. network router

LAB 12.2 CONFIGURING A USER ACCOUNT WITH RAS OPTIONS

Objectives

The goal of this lab is to configure RAS options for a user account requiring access to a RAS server. After a RAS server is installed, you must specify from which users the RAS server can accept a connection. For Windows 2000, authorization is determined by the dial-in properties on the user account. In addition, you can set the hours during which your users can log on to the domain. After completing this lab, you will be able to:

> Log on to the Lonestar domain with a domain administrator account

> Add the Active Directory Users and Computers snap-in

> Create a user account

> Update the security on the user account to provide dial-in access

> Update the logon hours permitted for the user account

Materials Required

This lab will require the following:

> Access to a member server by means of a domain administrator account

> A user account and password supplied by your instructor

Estimated completion time: **30 minutes**

ACTIVITY

1. Log on to the Lonestar domain using the **domain administrator** account and password provided by your instructor.

2. Click **Start**, click **Run**, type **MMC**, click **OK**, click **Console**, and then click **Add/Remove Snap-in**. Click **Add**, click **Active Directory Users and Computers**, click **Add**, click **Close**, and then click **OK**.

3. Click **Console**, click **Save As**, click **Desktop** in the Save in drop-down list, click in the **File name** text box, type **ManRAS**, and then click **Save**.

If a previous student saved the ManRAS, click Yes to resave the console.

4. Expand **Active Directory User and Computers**, expand **lonestar.lonestar.com**, click the **Users** folder, click **Action**, point to **New**, and then click **User**.

5. Type **Ras** in the First name text box, type *UserFML* in the Last name text box, (where *F* is the first initial, *M* is the middle initial, and *L* is the initial of your last name) type **Ras*UserFML*** for the user logon name, and then click **Next**.

6. Type **password** in the Password text box, press the **Tab** key, type **password** for confirmation, click the **User cannot change password** check box, click the **Password never expires** check box, click **Next**, review the settings for *RasUserFML*, and then click **Finish**.

7. Right-click **Ras*UserFML***, click **Properties**, click the **Dial-in** tab, click the **Allow access** option button, and then click **Apply**.

8. Click the **Account** tab, and then click **Logon Hours**. Your screen should resemble Figure 12-2.

9. Click the intersection of Sunday and Midnight (on the left side of the diagram), and then drag to the intersection of Saturday and 8:00 a.m.. Click the **Logon Denied** option button, click **OK**, click **Apply**, and then click **OK**.

10. Log off the **domain administrator** account. Log on with the **administrator** account.

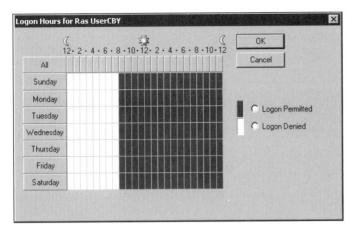

Figure 12-2   Logon hours setting

Certification Objectives

Objectives for Microsoft Exam 70-215: Installing, Configuring, and Administering Microsoft Windows 2000 Server:

➤ Configure hardware devices

➤ Install, configure, and troubleshoot a virtual private network

➤ Configure, monitor, and troubleshoot Remote Access

➤ Install, configure, and troubleshoot network protocols

Review Questions

1. Brian and Lillie discuss configuring user accounts for their future RAS users. They ask you to clarify the options that can be set from the Active Directory Users and Computers snap-in. Which of the following items will you include in your discussion with Brian and Lillie?

   a. permitted logon hours

   b. remote permissions for dial-out

   c. remote permissions for VPN

   d. remote computer for user logon

LAB 12.3 TEST ACCESS TO REMOTE ACCESS SERVER

Objectives

The goal of this lab is to create and test a connection to the RAS server with dial-up networking. You will create a dial-up connection with a RAS client. The RAS client makes a temporary, dial-up connection to a physical port on a RAS server. The best example of dial-up networking is a dial-up networking client that dials the phone number of one of the ports of a RAS server. After completing this lab, you will be able to:

➤ Launch the Phone and Modem Options applet from the Control Panel

➤ Install a modem

➤ Create a dial-in connection

➤ Test a dial-in connection by logging onto the RAS server

➤ Verify connection status

➤ Disconnect from a RAS server

Materials Required

This lab will require the following:

➤ Access to a second computer running Windows 2000 as a member server

➤ Completion of Labs 12.1 and 12.2.

Estimated completion time: **30 minutes**

ACTIVITY

1. Go to the second computer. Log on with the **administrator** account.

2. Complete Steps 2 through 4 from Lab 12.1 for the modem on the second computer.

3. Double-click **Network and Dial-up Connections** in the Control Panel, double-click **Make New Connection**, click **Next**, retain the **Dial-up to private network** option button, and then click **Next**.

4. Type *phonenumber* (where *phonenumber* is the number provided by your instructor), click **Next**, click **Next**, click **Next**, and then click **Finish**.

5. Type the **Ras*UserFML*** user account created in Lab 12.2, press **Tab**, and then type the *password* for the user account created in Lab 12.2. Click **Dial**.

6. View the **status** message boxes. When the connection is complete, click **OK**.

7. Right-click the **Dial-up connection** icon on the taskbar, click **Status**, verify the **connection time**, and then verify the **Sent and Received** activity.

8. Click the **Details** tab, verify the detailed information about the connection, including Server type, Transports, Authentication, Compression, and Server and Client IP address. Your screen should resemble Figure 12-3. Click **Close**.

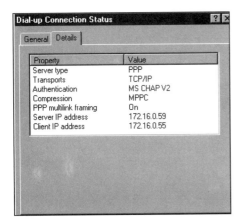

Figure 12-3   Dial-up connection details

9. Right-click the **Dial-up connection** icon, click **Disconnect**, close the **Network and Dial-up Connections** window, and then log off the **administrator** account.

Certification Objectives

Objectives for Microsoft Exam 70-215: Installing, Configuring, and Administering Microsoft Windows 2000 Server:

> ➤ Install, configure, and troubleshoot a virtual private network

> ➤ Configure, monitor, and troubleshoot Remote Access

> ➤ Install, configure, and troubleshoot network protocols

Review Questions

1. Which of the following properties can be viewed from the Details tab of the Dial-up Connection status window?
   a. Server type
   b. Transports
   c. Authentication
   d. Compression
   e. Client IP address

LAB 12.4 TEST ACCESS TO A VIRTUAL PRIVATE NETWORK SERVER

Objectives

The goal of this lab is to create a VPN client that can access the VPN server created in Lab 12.1. You will use VPN to encrypt and transfer critical data across a public network.

A VPN client uses special TCP/IP-based protocols called tunneling protocols. In this lab, a dial-up connection is established to the RAS server. Next, a virtual call is made to a virtual port on the VPN server. A VPN commonly occurs when a VPN client makes a VPN connection to a RAS server. The RAS server answers the virtual call, authenticates the caller, and transfers data between the VPN client and the network using the tunneling protocol. After completing this lab, you will be able to:

> ➤ Create a VPN connection

> ➤ Test the VPN connection by logging onto the VPN server

> ➤ Verify the connection status

Materials Required

This lab will require the following:

> ➤ Access to a computer running Windows 2000 as a member server

> ➤ Completion of Labs 12.1 and 12.2

Estimated completion time: **30 minutes**

Activity Background

In some environments, data is so sensitive that it must be physically separated and hidden. VPN connections provide this necessary isolation. Additionally, all communication across the VPN is encrypted for data confidentiality.

You can access a private network through the Internet, or other public network, by using a VPN connection with the Point-to-Point Tunneling Protocol (PPTP). PPTP enables the secure transfer of data from a remote computer to a private server by creating a VPN across TCP/IP-based data networks. PPTP supports dial-up virtual private networking over public networks, such as the Internet.

You can configure your dial-up VPN and direct connections to enforce various levels of password authentication and data encryption. Authentication methods range from unencrypted to custom encryption, such as the Extensible Authentication Protocol (EAP). In addition, the Internet Protocol Security (IPSec) options are supported by VPN. EAP provides flexible support for a wide range of authentication methods, including smart cards, certificates, one-time passwords, and public keys. You can also specify the type of data encryption, depending on the level of password authentication (MS CHAP or EAP) that you select. Finally, you can configure callback options to increase dial-up security.

ACTIVITY

1. Remain at the same computer at which you completed the previous lab. Log on with the **administrator** account.

2. Click **Start**, point to **Settings**, click **Control Panel**, double-click **Network and Dial-up Connections**, double-click **Make New Connection**, and then click **Next**.

3. Click **Connect to a private network through the Internet** option button, click **Next**, and then click **Next**.

4. Type *server* (where *server* is the name of the RAS server you created in Lab 12.1), click **Next**, click **Next**, click **Next**, and then click **Finish**.

5. Click **Yes** to the Initial Connection message.

6. Type **Ras***UserFML* (which is the user account created in Lab 12.2). Press the **Tab** key, type the **password** for the user account created in Lab 12.2, and then click **Dial** to complete the Dial-up connection.

7. View the **status** message boxes. When the connection is complete, click **OK**.

8. Type **Ras***UserFML* (which is the user account created in Lab 12.2). Press the **Tab** key, type the **password** for the user account created in Lab 12.2, and then click **Connect to complete the VPN connection.**

9. View the **status** message boxes. When the connection is complete, click **OK**.

10. Right-click the **Dial-up connection** icon on the taskbar, click **Status**, verify the **connection time**, and then verify the **Sent and Received** activity.

11. Click the **Details** tab, verify the detailed information about the connection, and then click **Close**.

12. Right-click the **Virtual Private Connection** icon on the taskbar, and then click **Status**.

13. Click the **Details** tab, verify the detailed information about the connection, and then click **Close**. Your screen should resemble Figure 12-4.

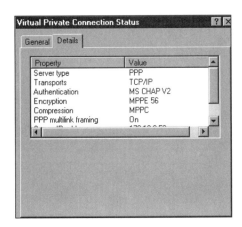

Figure 12-4   VPN connection details

14. Remain logged on with the VPN connection active.

Certification Objectives

Objectives for Microsoft Exam 70-215: Installing, Configuring, and Administering Microsoft Windows 2000 Server:

➤ Install, configure, and troubleshoot a virtual private network

➤ Configure, monitor, and troubleshoot Remote Access

➤ Install, configure, and troubleshoot network protocols

Review Questions

1. Indicate the correct sequence of steps to set up and test a VPN connection that is carried over a dial-in connection.

   1. Create a new dial-in connection for a private network.
   2. Dial the dial-in connection.
   3. Log on to the RAS server.
   4. Dial the VPN connection.
   5. Log on to the VPN connection.
   6. Access the RAS server through a secure connection.

   a. 1, 2, 3, 4, 5, 6
   b. 1, 2, 3, 5, 6
   c. 1, 4, 5, 6
   d. 1, 2, 4, 5, 6

2. Your boss asks you to prepare a short presentation about VPN connections. Which of the following will be on the list of notes for your presentation?

   a. A connection is established.
   b. VPN requires an Internet Service Provider (ISP).
   c. EAP supports the smart card.
   d. VPN packets are transported within PPTP.
   e. VPN requires MS CHAP V2 authentication.

LAB 12.5 REVIEW CONNECTIONS TO A REMOTE ACCESS SERVER

Objectives

The objective of this lab is to review the dial-in connections to the RAS server. As a network administrator, you will manage connections to your RAS server. In this lab, you will discover that the VPN connection is encapsulated within the dial-up connection. After completing this lab, you will be able to:

➤ Launch the Routing and Remote Access tool

➤ View the connection status for a dial-up connection

➤ View the connection status for a VPN connection

➤ Disconnect a VPN connection

➤ Disconnect a dial-up connection

Materials Required

This lab will require the following:

➤ Access to the VPN server created in Lab 12.1

➤ Completion of Lab 12.4

Estimated completion time: **30 minutes**

ACTIVITY

1. Move to the RAS created in Lab 12.1. Click **Start**, point to **Programs**, point to **Administrative Tools**, and then click **Routing and Remote Access**.

2. Expand *server* (where *server* is the name of the server created in Lab 12.1).

3. Click **Remote Access Clients** in the left pane, and then view the connections in the right pane. Your screen should resemble Figure 12-5.

12

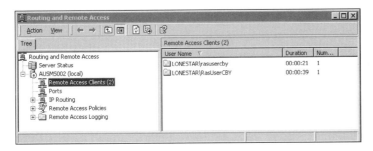

Figure 12-5   RAS connections

4. Right-click the **first connection**, view the status, and then click **Close**.

5. Right-click the **second connection**, view the status, and then click **Close**.

6. Click **Ports** in the left pane, right-click the **modem** connection, view the status, and then click **Close**.

7. Right-click the first **WAN Miniport** connection, view the status, and then click **Close**.

8. Right-click the first **WAN Miniport** connection, and then click **Disconnect**.

9. Click **Remote Access Clients** in the left pane, and then verify that one connection exists in the right pane.

10. Click **Ports** in the left pane, right-click the **modem** connection, and then click **Disconnect**.

11. Click **Remote Access Clients** in the left pane, and then verify that no connections exist in the right pane.

12. Close the **Routing and Remote Access** window, and then log off the computer. Return to the second computer, **close** all windows, and then log off from that computer as well.

Certification Objectives

Objectives for Microsoft Exam 70-215: Installing, Configuring, and Administering Microsoft Windows 2000 Server:

➤ Configure hardware devices

➤ Install, configure, and troubleshoot a virtual private network

➤ Configure, monitor, and troubleshoot Remote Access

➤ Install, configure, and troubleshoot network protocols

Review Questions

1. You get a call from a remote user. The user needs to know if a connection has been made to your AUSMS001 RAS. Indicate the correct sequence of steps to determine if the connection exists.

   1. Launch the Routing and Remote Access Server administrative tool.
   2. Launch CHKRAS from a command line.
   3. Select Server Status.
   4. Expand the AUSMS001(local).
   5. Select Remote Access Clients.
   6. View the connection status in the right pane.

   a. 2, 5, 6
   b. 1, 4, 5, 6
   c. 1, 3, 5, 6
   d. 1, 3, 4, 5, 6

2. You configured a RAS server using the RRAS administrative tool. You set up your first port for a modem. How many ports of each type were created?

   a. five PPTP, and five L2TP
   b. one modem
   c. one modem, five PPTP, and five L2TP
   d. one modem, three PPTP, and three L2TP
   e. none of the above

CHAPTER THIRTEEN

MANAGING INTERNET AND NETWORK INTEROPERABILITY

Labs included in this chapter

➤ Lab 13.1 Review IIS

➤ Lab 13.2 Create a Virtual Web Directory

➤ Lab 13.3 Installing Terminal Services for Remote Server Administration

➤ Lab 13.4 Testing Terminal Services for Remote Administration

➤ Lab 13.5 Using Telnet

Microsoft MCSE Exam #70-215 Objectives	
Objective	Lab
Install and configure network services for interoperability	13.1, 13.2, 13.3, 13.4, 13.5
Monitor, configure, troubleshoot, and control access to files, folders, and shared folders	13.1, 13.2
Install, configure, monitor, and troubleshoot Terminal Services	13.3, 13.4

LAB 13.1 REVIEW IIS

Objectives

The goal of this lab is to review IIS, which makes it easy for users in your organization to publish information on your intranet. After verifying that IIS is installed correctly, you will install the IIS snap-in. After completing this lab, you will be able to:

➤ Verify that the required subcomponents of IIS are installed

➤ Test connectivity to IIS with Internet Explorer

➤ Review pertinent IIS online documentation

➤ Add the IIS snap-in

Materials Required

This lab will require the following:

➤ Access to a computer running Windows 2000 Member Server

Estimated completion time: **30 minutes**

ACTIVITY

1. Log on to the member server with the **administrator** account.

2. Click **Start**, point to **Settings**, click **Control Panel**, and then double-click **Add/Remove Programs**.

3. Click **Add/Remove Windows Components**, click **Internet Information Services**, and then click **Details**. Observe the IIS subcomponents. Verify that the following subcomponents are checked: Common Files, Documentation, Internet Information Services IIS Snap-in, and World Wide Web Server. Click **OK**, click **Next**, click **Finish**, click **Close**, and then close the **Control Panel** window.

4. Click **Start**, click **Run**, type **http://localhost**, and then click **OK**.

If the Internet Connection has not been configured, click OK to start the Internet Connection Wizard. Click the I want to set up my Internet connection manually, or connect through a Local Area Network (LAN) option button. Click Next, click the I connect through a Local Area Network (LAN) option button, click Next, clear the Automatic discovery of proxy server check box, click Next, click No, click Next, and then click Finish.

5. Wait for the Welcome and Documentation pages to appear. Close the **Welcome** page.

6. In the **Documentation** page, expand **Administration**, expand **Web Site Management**, click **Creating Virtual Directories**, read the information about Creating Virtual Directories, and then close **Internet Explorer**.

7. Click **Start**, click **Run**, type **MMC**, click **OK**, click **Console**, click **Add/Remove Snap-in**, and then click **Add**. Scroll to find and then click **Internet Information Services Snap-in**, click **Add**, click **Close**, and then click **OK**.

8. Click **Console**, click **Save As**, click the **Save in** drop-down list, click **Desktop**, click the **File name** text box, type **ManIIS**, and then click **Save**.

If a previous student saved the ManIIS, click Yes to resave the console.

9. Remain logged on with the MMC open for the next lab.

Certification Objectives

Objectives for Microsoft Exam 70-215: Installing, Configuring, and Administering Microsoft Windows 2000 Server:

- Install and configure network services

- Monitor, configure, control, and troubleshoot access to Web sites

Review Questions

13

1. You are asked to present a brief overview of IIS, which consists of several subcomponents. Which subcomponents will you include in your overview?

   a. Cluster Service
   b. File Transfer Protocol (FTP)
   c. FrontPage 2000 Server Extensions
   d. NNTP Service
   e. Networking Services
   f. SMTP Service
   g. World Wide Web Server

LAB 13.2 CREATE A VIRTUAL WEB DIRECTORY

Objectives

The goal of this lab is to create a Virtual Web Directory for IIS. If your Web site contains files that are located on a directory other than the home directory, or on other computers, you must create virtual directories to include those files on your Web site. After completing this lab, you will be able to:

➤ Create a subdirectory for a Virtual Web Directory

➤ Create a Virtual Web Directory

➤ Apply permissions to a Virtual Web Directory

➤ Create a default Web page to test the Virtual Web Directory

➤ Launch Internet Explorer to view the default Web page

Materials Required

This lab will require the following:

➤ Access to the computer from Lab 13.1 that was running Windows 2000 Member Server

➤ Completion of Lab 13.1

Estimated completion time: **30 minutes**

Activity

1. Open the **MMC**, if necessary. Log on to the member server using the **administrator** account. Display the **Microsoft Management Console** (MMC).

2. Click **Start**, point to **Programs**, point to **Accessories**, click **Windows Explorer**, double-click **My Computer**, and then double-click **Local Disk (C:)**.

3. Right-click in the whitespace in the right pane. Point to **New**, click **Folder**, type *WebFML* (where *F* is your first initial, *M* is your middle initial, and *L* is your initial for your last name), and then close **Windows Explorer**.

4. Return to the **MMC**. Expand **Internet Information Services**, and then expand *server* (where *server* is the computer you used in Lab 13.1). Right-click **Default Web Site**, point to **New**, and then click **Virtual Directory**, as shown in Figure 13-1, to start the Virtual Directory Creation Wizard. Click **Next**.

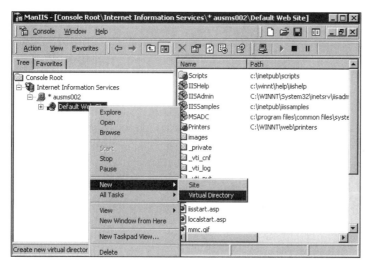

Figure 13-1 Selecting Virtual Directory

5. Type *WebFML*, click **Next**, click **Browse**, expand **Local Disk (C:)**, click the folder created in Step 3, click **OK**, click **Next**, click **Next,** and then click **Finish**.

6. Expand **Default Web Site**. Right-click *WebFML*, point to **All Tasks**, click **Permissions Wizard**, click **Next**, do not change the Inherit all security settings option button, and then click **Next**.

7. Review the Windows 2000 directory and file permissions that are recommended for your site. Do not deselect the Replace all directory and file permissions option button. Click **Next**, review the security summary, click **Next**, and then click **Finish**.

8. Click **Start**, point to **Programs**, point to **Accessories**, and then click **Notepad**.

9. Type the following lines of HTML:

   <HTML>
   <HEAD><TITLE>This is my default homepage.</TITLE></HEAD>
   <BODY>
   <H1>Welcome to my homepage</H1>
   <HR>
   This site is under construction!
   </BODY>
   </HTML>

10. Click **File** on the menu bar, click **Save As**, click the **Save as type** drop-down list, click **All Files**, click the **Save in** drop-down list, select **Local Disk (C:)**, double-click *WebFML*, type **default.htm** in the File name text box, click **Save**, and then minimize **Notepad**.

11. Click **Start**, click **Run**, type **http://localhost/WebFML**, and then verify that you get your default Web page.

If you did not get your default Web page, ask your instructor for assistance.

12. Close all open applications. Click **Yes** to the Save console settings to ManIIS? message, and then log off the computer.

Certification Objectives

Objectives for Microsoft Exam 70-215: Installing, Configuring, and Administering Microsoft Windows 2000 Server:

➤ Install and configure network services

➤ Monitor, configure, control, and troubleshoot access to Web sites

➤ Monitor, configure, troubleshoot, and control access to files and folders via Web services

Review Questions

1. IIS is installed on the AUSMS003 Windows 2000 server. Which of the following would be the correct locations for a Virtual Web Directory? (Choose all correct answers.)

   a. c:\winnt

   b. d:\sales

   c. \\ausms004\sales

   d. d:\inetpub\wwwroot

   e. d:\Web\budget

2. What is the correct sequence of steps to create a Virtual Web Directory on a Windows 2000 member server with the IIS snap-in?

   1. Open MMC with IIS snap-in.
   2. Start the Virtual Directory Wizard.
   3. Locate the existing folder for the Web pages.
   4. Launch Internet Explorer.
   5. Create a folder for the Web pages.

   a. 1, 2, 3, 4, 5

   b. 1, 2, 4, 5, 3

   c. 4, 5, 1, 2, 3

   d. 1, 4, 2, 3, 5

3. You plan to implement a new IIS server. The HTML pages are stored at locations on multiple servers. You establish the following goals for the Web server:

   1. Permit the Sales organization to update its own pages on the AUSMS005 server.
   2. Restrict access for the Sales pages to the Sales group.
   3. Permit the Tech group to update their Web pages.
   4. Permit all persons access to the Tech group's Tech News and IIS documentation.

   You will create virtual directories for Sales and Tech. For the Sales directory, you will use \\AUSMS005\Sales where Sales is the share name with the default share permissions. For the Tech directory, you will use e:\tech. NTFS permissions restrict updates for the e:\tech folder to the Tech group. For the documentation, you will use d:\inetpub\wwwroot. You ask Peter to review your plan. Which of the following will Peter say?

   a. Goal 1 is met.

   b. Goal 2 is met.

   c. Goal 3 is met.

   d. Goal 4 is met.

   e. No goals are met.

LAB 13.3 INSTALL TERMINAL SERVICES FOR REMOTE SERVER ADMINISTRATION

13

Objectives

The goal of this lab is to install Terminal Services, which provides remote access to a server desktop through a client serving as a terminal emulator. Terminal Services transmits only the GUI interface to the client. The client then returns keyboard and mouse clicks to the server for processing. When used for remote administration, Terminal Services provides remote access for administering your server from other computers on your network. After completing this lab, you will be able to:

➤ Install Terminal Services

➤ Configure Terminal Services to disable the Active Desktop

➤ Create the Terminal Services Client disks

Materials Required

This lab will require the following:

➤ Access to a computer running Windows 2000 Member Server

➤ The Windows 2000 Server CD-ROM

➤ Two blank, formatted disks

Estimated completion time: **45 minutes**

Activity

1. Log on to a member server with the **administrator** account.

2. Click **Start**, point to **Settings**, click **Control Panel**, and then double-click **Add/Remove Programs.**

3. Click **Add/Remove Windows Components**, and then find and check the **Terminal Services** check box.

Click OK to the Offline Files is not compatible with Terminal Services message, if it appears.

4. Click **Next**, accept the default mode, as shown in Figure 13-2, and then click **Next**.

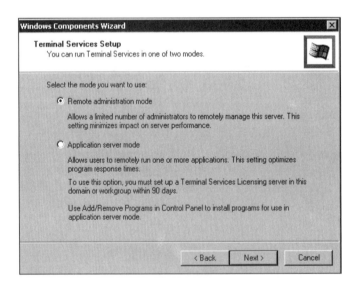

Figure 13-2   Terminal Services Setup

5. When requested, insert the Windows 2000 Server CD-ROM, click **Exit**, click **OK**, and wait for the files to copy. Click **Finish**, close any open applications, remove the Windows 2000 Server CD-ROM, and then click **Yes** to restart the computer.

When installing additional Windows 2000 Server components, click Browse to locate the CD-ROM. This is useful if the drive letter was changed after the initial installation of Windows 2000 Server.

6. Log on with the **administrator** account.

7. Click **Start**, point to **Programs**, point to **Administrative Tools**, click **Terminal Services Configuration**, click **Server Settings**, right-click **Active Desktop** in the right pane, and then click **Disable**, as shown in Figure 13-3. Close the **Terminal Services Configuration** window.

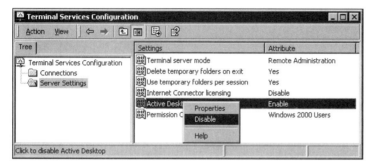

Figure 13-3   Disable option

8. Click **Start**, point to **Programs**, point to **Administrative Tools**, click **Terminal Services Client Creator**, click **Terminal Services for 32-bit x86 windows**, and then click **Format disk(s)**.

9. Insert the first blank disk, click **OK**, click **OK**, and then click **Yes** to the This operation will erase all data on destination disk message. Wait for first disk to be formatted and copied, remove the first disk, and then label the disk **TS client #1**.

10. Insert second disk, click **OK**, click **Yes** to This operation will erase all data on destination disk message. Wait for second disk to be formatted and copied, remove the second disk, and then label the disk **TS client #2**. Click **OK**, and then click **Cancel**.

11. Click **Start**, point to **Programs**, point to **Administrative Tools**, click **Terminal Services Manager**, click **OK** to the Certain features such as Remote Control... message, expand *server*, and then observe the connections.

12. Remain logged on to this computer. Go to a second computer for the next lab.

Certification Objectives

Objectives for Microsoft Exam 70-215: Installing, Configuring, and Administering Microsoft Windows 2000 Server:

➤ Install and configure network services

➤ Install, configure, monitor, and troubleshoot Terminal Services

➤ Remotely administer servers by using Terminal Services

➤ Configure Terminal Services for application sharing

➤ Configure applications for use with Terminal Services

Review Questions

1. Brian and Lillie discuss the salient issues regarding Terminal Services. They ask you about the key points. Which of the following will you include in your discussion with Brian and Lillie?

   a. Terminal Services provides remote access to a server desktop.

   b. Terminal Services can use any terminal emulator supplied with Windows 2000 Professional.

   c. Terminal Services transmits only changes from the desktop interface to the client.

   d. The client returns keyboard and mouse clicks to be processed by the server.

   e. Terminal Services provides remote access for administering your server from other computers on your network.

   f. Terminal Services functions simultaneously in both remote administration and application modes.

2. Leonard is concerned about the proper steps to create the Terminal Services Client. He prepared a list of steps. He asks you about the correct sequence of steps. Indicate the correct steps and sequence.

   1. Open the Administrative Tools menu.
   2. Select Terminal Services for 32-bit x86 windows.
   3. Launch Terminal Services Client.
   4. Select Format disk(s).
   5. Insert the first disk.
   6. Remove the first disk, and then insert the second disk.

   a. 3, 2, 4, 5, 6

   b. 1, 2, 3, 4, 5, 6

   c. 1, 3, 2, 4, 5, 6

   d. 1, 3, 4, 2, 5, 6

LAB 13.4 TEST TERMINAL SERVICES FOR REMOTE ADMINISTRATION

Objectives

The goal of this lab is to test Terminal Services for remote administration of a Windows 2000 server. The Terminal Services Client connects to the Windows 2000 server that is running Terminal Services. As a network administrator, this provides you with a method of remotely managing your server over the network from any client computer. After completing this lab you will be able to:

➤ Install the Terminal Services Client

➤ Launch the Terminal Services Client

➤ Connect to the Terminal Services computer

➤ View a folder on the Terminal Services computer

➤ Send a message to the Terminal Services Client computer

➤ View a message sent from the Terminal Services computer

➤ Disconnect a remote client from the Terminal Services computer

➤ View the connection results on the Terminal Services Client computer

➤ Disable Terminal Services on the first computer

Materials Required

This lab will require the following:

➤ Access to a computer running Windows 2000 Member Server

➤ The two Terminal Services Client disks created in Lab 13.3

Estimated completion time: **30 minutes**

Activity

1. Log on with the **administrator** account. Insert the first disk, click **Start**, click **Run**, type **a:\setup.exe**, and then click **OK**. If prompted, click the **Reinstall** button to repeat the last installation.

> If this is first Terminal Services Client installation, click Continue, type your name, click OK, click OK, click the I Agree to accept the EULA option button, and then click the Terminal Services Client install button.

2. Click **Yes**. Wait for the first disk to be copied, remove the first disk, and then insert the second disk. Click **OK**, and then click **OK**.

3. Click **Start**, point to **Programs**, point to **Terminal Services Client**, click **Terminal Services Client**, locate and click *server* in the Available servers list, as shown in Figure 13-4, and then click **Connect**. Log on to the first computer from the Terminal Services Client window.

13

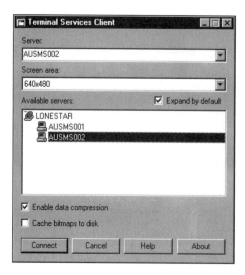

Figure 13-4   Connecting to Terminal Services

4. Scroll in the Terminal Services Client window to view the desktop on the first computer. Click **Start**, point to **Programs**, point to **Accessories**, click **Window Explorer**, double-click **My Computer**, double- click **Local Disk (C:)**, and then view the directory contents of the first computer.

5. Remain logged on with the Terminal Services Client window open.

6. Return to the first computer. View the remote connections, as shown in Figure 13-5.

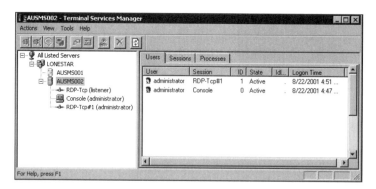

Figure 13-5   Connections to Terminal Services clients

7. Right-click the connection to the second computer, click **Send Message**, but do not change the Message Title. Type **Stopping Terminal Services in 30 seconds** in the message area, and then click **OK**.

8. Return to the second computer, and then click **OK** to the Stopping Terminal Services in 30 seconds message.

9. Return to the first computer. Right-click the connection to the second computer, click **Disconnect**, and then click **OK** to the Each selected session will be disconnected message.

10. Return to the second computer. Click **Close** to the Terminal Server has ended the connection message. Close the **Terminal Services Client** window. Close any open applications and log off.

11. Return to the first computer. Close the **Terminal Services Manager** window.

12. Click **Start**, point to **Settings**, click **Control Panel**, double-click **Add/Remove Programs**, and then click **Add/Remove Windows Components**. Scroll to and clear the **Terminal Services** check box, click **Next**, click **Finish**, close any open applications, and then click **Yes** to restart the computer.

Certification Objectives

Objectives for Microsoft Exam 70-215: Installing, Configuring, and Administering Microsoft Windows 2000 Server:

➤ Install and configure network services

➤ Install, configure, monitor, and troubleshoot Terminal Services

➤ Remotely administer servers by using Terminal Services

➤ Configure Terminal Services for application sharing

➤ Configure applications for use with Terminal Services

Review Questions

1. You plan to manage your Windows 2000 servers from your existing Windows NT workstations. You established the following goals:

   1. Access Windows 2000 application servers for remote administration.
   2. Access remaining Windows 2000 servers for remote administration.
   3. Use existing Windows NT workstations.
   4. Permit all five network administrators to access servers simultaneously.

   You will install Terminal Services in the application mode on the Windows 2000 application servers. You plan to install Terminal Services in the remote mode on the remaining Windows 2000 servers. You create the Terminal Services for 32-bit *x*86 windows disks. You will install the Terminal Services Client on your five existing Windows NT workstations. Since you are not running applications with Terminal Services on the application servers, you decide that you don't need to purchase Terminal Services licenses. You ask Joan to review your plan. What will Joan say about your plan?

   a. Goal 1 is met.

   b. Goal 2 is met.

   c. Goal 3 is met.

d. Goal 4 is met.

e. No goals are met.

LAB 13.5 USE TELNET

Objectives

The goal of this lab is to configure the Telnet service, and test access to the Telnet server from a second computer. Windows 2000 Telnet Server allows Telnet clients to connect to a server, log on to that server, and run data management commands. You will be able to use the Telnet client to efficiently manage the data on a remote server. For example, you can view the directory structure on a remote server. After completing this lab, you will be able to:

➤ Configure and start the Telnet service

➤ Launch a Command Prompt window

➤ Test the Telnet service with the Telnet client

➤ Use the Telnet Server administration tool

Materials Required

This lab will require the following:

➤ Access to two computers running Windows 2000 Member Server

Estimated completion time: **30 minutes**

Activity

1. Log on to the first member server as **administrator**.

2. Click **Start**, point to **Programs**, point to **Administrative Tools**, click **Services**, scroll to locate and then right-click **Telnet**, click **Properties**, click the **Startup type** drop-down list, click **Automatic**, click **Apply**, click **Start**, and then click **OK**.

3. Go to the second computer. Log on as an **administrator**. Click **Start**, point to **Programs**, point to **Accessories**, click **Command Prompt**, type **telnet** *server* (where *server* is the name of the server in Step 2), press **Enter**, wait for the Welcome to Microsoft Telnet Server window to appear, type **dir**, press **Enter**, and then view the subdirectory listing for the first computer.

4. Return to the first computer. Click **Start**, point to **Programs**, point to **Administrative Tools**, click **Telnet Server Administration**, type **1**, press **Enter**, and then observe the SESSION ID. Type **2**, press **Enter**, type *n* (where *n* is the SESSION ID), press **Enter**, type **0**, and then press **Enter**.

5. Return to the second computer. Locate the **Command Prompt** window. Observe the Connection to host lost message. Type **Exit**, press **Enter**, close any open applications, and then log off the computer.

6. Return to the first computer. Make the **Services** window visible on your screen. Right-click **Telnet**, click **Properties**, click the **Startup type** drop-down list, click **Manual**, click **Apply**, click **Stop**, and then click **OK**.

7. Close any open applications. Log off the computer.

Certification Objectives

Objectives for Microsoft Exam 70-215: Installing, Configuring, and Administering Microsoft Windows 2000 Server:

➤ Install and configure network services

Review Questions

1. George calls you about the Windows 2000 Server Telnet service. George has questions about the tasks that the Telnet client can perform on a remote server. You make a list of items to discuss prior to your meeting later today. What items will you include on your list?

   a. connects to remote hosts

   b. enables the viewing of subdirectories

   c. edits text files with EDIT.COM

   d. creates subdirectories

   e. launches Windows applications

2. Brian and Rose discuss the steps to control a Windows 2000 service. Brian prepared a list of steps. They ask you about the correct sequence of steps. Indicate the correct steps and sequence.

   1. Open the Administrative Tools menu.
   2. Launch Services.
   3. Right-click the indicated service.
   4. Click Automatic.
   5. Click Properties.
   6. Select Apply.
   7. Select Start.

   a. 1, 3, 4, 5, 6

   b. 1, 2, 3, 5, 4, 7, 6

   c. 1, 2, 3, 5, 4, 6, 7

   d. 1, 2, 3, 5, 6

13

CHAPTER FOURTEEN

SERVER MONITORING AND OPTIMIZATION

Labs included in this chapter

➤ Lab 14.1 Install System Monitor

➤ Lab 14.2 Disk Optimization

➤ Lab 14.3 Memory Management

➤ Lab 14.4 Processor Utilization

➤ Lab 14.5 Establish a Baseline

➤ Lab 14.6 Examine Processor Alert

Microsoft MCSE Exam #70-215 Objectives	
Objective	Lab
Monitor and optimize usage of system resources	14.1, 14.2, 14.3, 14.4, 14.5, 14.6
Manage processes	14.1, 14.2, 14.5, 14.6
Optimize disk performance	14.1, 14.2, 14.5, 14.6
Manage and optimize availability of system state and user data	14.1

LAB 14.1 INSTALL SYSTEM MONITOR

Objectives

The goal of this lab is to install and use System Monitor. As a network administrator, you will monitor system performance so that you can recognize bottlenecks on your servers. A bottleneck is a condition in which an activity prevents a resource from performing at its best. Network administrators who neglect the monitoring of system performance will find servers are not sharing workloads, settings are not configured optimally, and servers do not have sufficient resources.

With System Monitor, you will use the following performance data to perform disk optimization, manage memory, and find processor bottlenecks:

➤ % Processor Time provides a measure of how much time the processor actually spends working on productive threads versus how often it is busy servicing requests. A measure consistently over 85 percent indicates a bottleneck.

➤ Pages/sec is a general indicator of how often the system uses the hard drive to store or retrieve memory-associated data. If you have a value over 20, you need to analyze paging activity.

➤ % Disk Time is a general indicator of how busy the disk is. Note that the disk could cause a bottleneck prior to the % Disk Time reaching 100 percent.

After completing this lab, you will be able to:

➤ Launch the Performance application

➤ Create and save a console for the System Monitor

➤ Add Performance counters (% Processor Time, Pages/sec, and % Disk Time)

➤ Simulate various kinds of activity

➤ Interpret the System Monitor graph

Materials Required

This lab will require the following:

➤ Access to a computer running Windows 2000 Member Server

Estimated completion time: **15 minutes**

ACTIVITY

1. Log on as an **administrator** to a member server.

2. Click **Start**, point to **Programs**, point to **Administrative Tools**, and then click **Performance**. Your screen should resemble Figure 14-1.

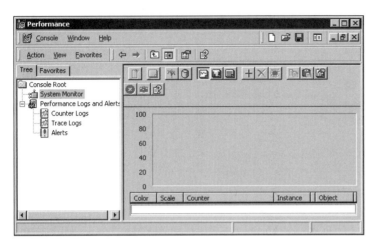

Figure 14-1   System Monitor layout

3. Click **Console**, click **Save As**, click the **Save in** drop-down list, click **Desktop**, click the **File name** text box, type **Monitor**, and then click **Save**.

 If a previous student saved the System Monitor, click Yes to resave the console.

4. Click **System Monitor Add** button (it resembles a plus + sign) to open the Add Counters dialog box.

14

 To determine an action for the buttons displayed on the toolbar for System Monitor, place the mouse over the button. For example, placing the mouse over the + button will display "Add," which indicates the System Monitor Add button.

5. Click the **Use local computer counters** option button. Your screen should resemble Figure 14-2. Click the **Performance object** drop-down list. Scroll to find and then click **Processor**. Click the **Select counters from list** option button, scroll to find and then click **% Processor Time**. Click **_Total** from the instances list, click **Explain**, read the explanation for the counter, and then click **Add**.

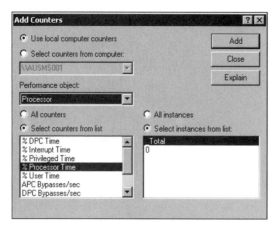

Figure 14-2   Selecting counters

 Click Explain to see an explanation of the various objects and counters. This is a real time saver when looking for a counter.

6. Click the **Performance object** drop-down list. Scroll to find and then click **Memory**. Scroll to find and then click **Pages/sec** from the Select counters from list. Read the explanation for the counter, and then click **Add**.

7. Click the **Performance object** drop-down list. Scroll to find and then click **PhysicalDisk.** Scroll to find and then click **% Disk Time**, and then click **0 C:**. (Note that your disk selection display may look different.) Read the explanation for the counter, click **Add**, and then click **Close**.

8. Move the **Performance** window to simulate activity. Observe the changes in the graph.

 You can expand the Counter column heading (located between the Scale column and Instance column) to reveal the full counter titles.

9. Click **Start**, point to **Search**, click **Search For Files and Folders**, and then type **EXE** in the Search for files or folders named text box. Click the **Look in** drop-down list, and then click **Local Harddrives (C:)**, as shown in Figure 14-3.

Figure 14-3   Searching for files

10. Click the **Search Now** button, minimize the **Search Results** window, and then observe the changes in % Processor Time and Pages/sec in the Performance window.

11. Restore the **Search Results** window. Clear the **Search for Files and Folders named** text box, type **lonestar** in the Containing text text box, and then click **Search Now**. Minimize the **Search Results** window.

12. Observe the changes in Pages/sec and % Disk Time counters in the Performance window, as illustrated in Figure 14-4.

14

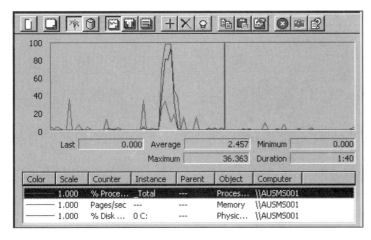

Figure 14-4   Sample performance counters

13. Restore the **Search Results** window, click **Stop Search**, and then close the Search Results window.

14. Click the **Highlight** button (it resembles a light bulb), and then click **% Processor Time** to highlight the line in the graph.

> You may want to change the displayed scale of a selected counter in the graph. Counter values can be scaled exponentially from .0000001 to 1000000. If the lines lack visibility, you may want to adjust the counter scale settings. Changing the scale does not affect the statistics displayed in the value bar. To change the scale, right-click the right pane, click Properties, click the Data tab, click the counter, click the Scale drop-down list, click the scaling factor, click Apply, and then click OK.

15. Click the **New Counter Set** button (the leftmost button on the toolbar) to stop the graph.

16. Close the **Performance** window, and then click **Yes** to save console settings.

17. Remain logged on for the next lab.

Certification Objectives

Objectives for Microsoft Exam 70-215: Installing, Configuring, and Administering Microsoft Windows 2000 Server:

➤ Monitor and optimize use of system resources

➤ Manage processes

➤ Optimize disk performance

➤ Manage and optimize availability of system and user data

Review Questions

1. Michael asks you to provide the correct sequence of steps to set up a System Monitor session. Which answer indicates the correct sequence of steps to add the % Processor Time, Pages/sec, and % Disk Time counters?

   1. Click the Add Counter button.
   2. Click the Use local computer counters button.
   3. Select the Processor object.
   4. Select the Memory object.
   5. Select the PhysicalDisk object.
   6. Select % Processor Time.
   7. Select Pages/sec.
   8. Select % Disk Time.
   9. Click Add.
   10. Click Close.

    a. 1, 2, 3, 6, 4, 7, 5, 8, 9, 10

    b. 1, 2, 3, 7, 9, 4, 7, 9, 5, 8, 9, 10

    c. 1, 2, 3, 3, 6, 4, 7, 5, 8, 10

    d. 1, 2, 3, 6, 9, 4, 7, 9, 5, 8, 9, 10

2. Georgia noticed that % Processor Time is consistently over 85 percent on a Windows 2000 server on her network. What should she do to solve this problem?

    a. Add more RAM.

    b. Add a second processor to the dual-processor system board.

    c. Replace the processor with a faster processor.

    d. Increase the size of the paging file.

LAB 14.2 DISK OPTIMIZATION

Objectives

The goal of this lab is to monitor access to disks on your server. Disk usage statistics help you balance the workload of your servers. System Monitor provides physical disk counters for troubleshooting, capacity planning, and measuring activity on a physical volume. In this lab, you will set up the following Microsoft-recommended physical disk counters:

➤ Disk Reads/sec is the number of reads that the disk can accomplish per second. This should be below the manufacturer's specifications for the disk drive.

➤ Disk Writes/sec is the number of writes that the disk can accomplish per second. As with the Disk Reads/sec, this should be below the manufacturer's specifications for the disk drive.

➤ Current Disk Queue Length provides the number of system requests that are waiting for disk access. This number should remain steady at no more than two.

➤ Disk Time is a general indicator of how busy the disk is. If the value of the counter rises to more than 90 percent, check the Current Disk Queue Length.

In addition, the % Free Space, which is a logical disk counter, is useful for monitoring the percentage of available free space on a volume. After completing this lab, you will be able to:

➤ Launch a Command Prompt window

➤ Review the command line options for diskperf

➤ Configure the disk performance statistics driver with diskperf

➤ Add physical and logical disk counters to a graph

➤ Simulate various kinds of activity

➤ Interpret the System Monitor graph

14

Materials Required

This lab will require the following:

➤ Access to a computer running Windows 2000 Member Server

➤ Completion of Lab 14.1

Estimated completion time: **15 minutes**

ACTIVITY

1. You should be logged on as administrator. Click **Start**, point to **Programs**, point to **Accessories**, click **Command Prompt**, and then type **diskperf /?**. Press **Enter**, and then read the options displayed.

2. Type **diskperf –Y**, press **Enter**, type **exit**, and then press **Enter**.

3. To enable the disk performance counters, close any open windows, point to **Start**, click **Shutdown**, click the **What do you want to do?** drop-down list, select **Restart**, and then click **OK**.

4. Log on as an **administrator**. Double-click the **Monitor** icon on the desktop to open the System Monitor.

5. Click the **Add Counter** button to open the Add Counters dialog box, and then click the **Use local computer counters** option button.

6. Click the **Performance object** drop-down list. Scroll to find and then click **PhysicalDisk**. Scroll to find and then click **% Disk Time**. Click **0 C:** (your display may differ), click **Explain**, read the explanation for the counter, and then click **Add**.

7. Repeat Step 6 for Disk Reads/sec, Disk Writes/sec, and Current Disk Queue Length.

8. Click the **Performance object** drop-down list. Scroll to find and then click **LogicalDisk**. Scroll to find and then click **% Free Space**, click **C:**, read the explanation for the counter, click **Add**, and then click **Close**.

9. Click **Start**, point to **Search**, click **Search for Files and Folders**, type **EXE** in the Search for files or folders named text box, click the **Look in** drop-down list, click **Local Harddrives**, click **Search Now**, and then minimize the **Search Results** window.

10. Observe the changes in the counters.

11. Restore the **Search Results** window. Clear the **Search for Files and Folders named** text box, type **lonestar** in the Containing text text box, click **Search Now**, and then minimize the **Search Results** window.

12. Observe the changes in the counters. Click the **% Disk Time** counter, and then observe the statistics (Last, Average, Minimum, Maximum, and Duration).

13. Repeat Step 12 for the remaining counters.

 To change the characteristics of the lines in the graph, right-click the right pane, click Properties, click the Data tab, click the counter, click the Color drop-down list and make a selection, click the Width of style drop-down list and make a selection, click Apply, and then click OK.

14. To change the view to a chart, click the **View Histogram** button.

15. To change the view to a report, click the **View Report** button.

16. Click the **View Graph** button.

17. Click the **New Counter Set** button (the leftmost button on toolbar) to stop the graph.

18. Close the **Search Results** window. Leave the Performance window open and remain logged on for the next lab.

Certification Objectives

Objectives for Microsoft Exam 70-215: Installing, Configuring, and Administering Microsoft Windows 2000 Server:

➤ Monitor and optimize use of system resources

➤ Manage processes

➤ Optimize disk performance

➤ Manage and optimize availability of system and user data

14

Review Questions

1. Brian and Lillie try to determine which diskperf switch to use with logical disk counters. Which switch will you tell Brian and Lillie to use?
   a. Diskperf.exe –Y
   b. Diskperf.exe /?
   c. Diskperf.exe /YV
   d. Diskperf.exe –YV

2. Jill noticed that % Disk Time is consistently over 90 percent on a Windows 2000 server on her network. What should she do to solve this problem?
   a. Replace the hard drive.
   b. Verify that the number of Disk Reads/sec is below the manufacture's specifications.

    c. Verify that the number of Disk Writes/sec is below the manufacture's specifications.

    d. Verify that the Current Disk Queue Length is no more than two.

LAB 14.3 MEMORY MANAGEMENT

Objectives

The goal of this lab is to monitor memory usage on your server. If your system is paging frequently, you may have a memory shortage. Although some paging is acceptable because it enables Windows 2000 to use more memory than actually exists, constant paging is a drain on system performance.

Reducing paging will significantly improve system responsiveness. In this lab, you will set up the following counters that are recommended for memory and paging:

> ➤ Available Mbytes indicates the amount of memory that is left after operating system allocations. Should it drop below 4 MB or 5 percent of RAM memory for a sustained period, on the order of minutes at a time, there may be a memory shortage.

> ➤ Cache Bytes monitors the number of bytes used by the file system cache. Use this counter in conjunction with Available Mbytes. If the value rises above 4 MB, you may need to add more RAM memory.

> ➤ Pages/sec is a general indicator of how often the system uses the hard drive to store or retrieve memory-associated data. If you have a value over 20, you need to analyze paging activity.

> ➤ PageFaults/sec gives a general idea of how often requested information must be retrieved from another location in memory, or from the page file. Although a sustained value may indicate trouble here, you should be more concerned with hard page faults that represent actual reads or writes to the disk. Remember that the disk access is much slower than RAM.

> ➤ Usage Paging File should be reviewed if you suspect that paging is a bottleneck. The acceptable threshold for this value is 99 percent.

After completing this lab, you will be able to:

> ➤ Add physical counters to a graph

> ➤ Simulate various kinds of activity

> ➤ Interpret the System Monitor graph

Materials Required

This lab will require the following:

➤ Access to a computer running Windows 2000 Member Server

➤ Completion of Labs 14.1 and 14.2

Estimated completion time: **15 minutes**

ACTIVITY

1. You should be logged on as administrator with the Performance window open. Click the **Add Counter** button to open the Add Counters dialog box, and then click the **Use local computer counters** option button.

2. Click the **Performance object** drop-down list. Scroll to find and then click **Memory.** Scroll to find and then click **Pages/sec**, click **Explain**, read the explanation for the counter, and then click **Add**.

3. Repeat Step 2 for Available MBytes, Cache Bytes, and Page Faults/sec.

4. Click the **Performance object** drop-down list. Scroll to find and then click **Paging File**, scroll to find and then click **% Usage**, click **_Total**, and then read the explanation for the counter. Click **Add**, and then click **Close**.

5. Click **Start**, point to **Search**, click **Search for Files and Folders**, type **lonestar** in the Containing text text box, click the **Look in** drop-down list, click **Local Harddrives (C:)**, click **Search Now**, and then minimize the **Search Results** window.

6. Observe the changes in the counters, click the **Pages/sec** counter, and then observe the statistics (Last, Average, Minimum, Maximum, and Duration).

7. Repeat Step 6 for the remaining counters.

8. Click the **New Counter Set** button (the leftmost button on the toolbar) to stop the graph.

9. Close the **Search Results** window. Leave the Performance window open and remain logged on for the next lab.

14

Certification Objectives

Objectives for Microsoft Exam 70-215: Installing, Configuring, and Administering Microsoft Windows 2000 Server:

➤ Monitor and optimize use of system resources

➤ Manage processes

➤ Optimize disk performance

➤ Manage and optimize availability of system and user data

Review Questions

1. George noticed that Pages/sec is higher than normal on a Windows 2000 server on his network. What should George do to solve this problem?

   a. Add more RAM.

   b. Increase the size of the paging file.

   c. Move the paging file to the volume that contains the system files.

   d. Reduce the size of the paging file.

2. Peter is monitoring Available MBytes and Cache Bytes with System Monitor on a Windows 2000 server. When should Peter be concerned?

   a. when Available MBytes exceeds 4 MB

   b. when Available MBytes falls below 4 MB

   c. when Cache Bytes exceeds 4 MB

   d. when Cache Bytes falls below 4 MB

Lab 14.4 Processor Utilization

Objectives

The goal of this lab is to monitor processor usage on your server. Monitoring the Processor and System object counters provides valuable information about the utilization of your processors. You must have this information to effectively tune your application servers. You will want to monitor with the following counters: % Processor Time, Interrupts/sec, and Processor Queue Length for bottleneck detection. After completing this lab, you will be able to:

➤ Add physical counters to a graph

➤ Simulate various kinds of activity

➤ Interpret the System Monitor graph

Materials Required

This lab will require the following:

➤ Access to a computer running Windows 2000 Member Server

➤ Completion of Labs 14.1, 14.2, and 14.3

Estimated completion time: **15 minutes**

ACTIVITY

1. You should be logged on as administrator with the Performance window open. Click the **Add Counter** button to open the Add Counters dialog box, and then click the **Use local computer counters** option button.

2. Click the **Performance object** drop-down list. Scroll to find and then click **Processor**. Scroll to find and then click **% Processor Time**, click **_Total**, click **Explain**, read the explanation for the counter, click **Add**, and then click **Interrupts/sec**. Click **_Total**, read the explanation for the counter, and then click **Add**.

3. Click the **Performance object** drop-down list. Scroll to find and then click **System**. Scroll to find and then click **Processor Queue Length**, read the explanation for the counter, click **Add**, and then click **Close**.

4. Click **Start**, point to **Search**, click **Search for files and folders**, type **lonestar** in the Containing text text box, click the **Look in** drop-down list, click **Local Harddrives (C:)**, click **Search Now**, and then minimize the **Search Results** window.

5. Observe the changes in the counters, click the **% Processor Time** counter, and then observe the statistics (Last, Average, Minimum, Maximum, and Duration).

6. Repeat Step 6 for the remaining counters.

7. Click the **New Counter Set** button (the leftmost button on the toolbar) to stop the graph.

8. Close the **Search Results** window. Leave the Performance window open and remain logged on for the next lab.

Certification Objectives

14

Objectives for Microsoft Exam 70-215: Installing, Configuring, and Administering Microsoft Windows 2000 Server:

➤ Monitor and optimize use of system resources

➤ Manage processes

➤ Optimize disk performance

➤ Manage and optimize availability of system and user data

Review Questions

1. Roberta wants to determine whether processor activity is excessive on her Windows 2000 server. Which counters should she monitor?
   a. System Object: Processor Queue Length and % Processor Time
   b. % Processor Time and % Usage

    c. % Usage and Interrupts/sec

    d. System Object: Processor Queue Length and % Usage

2. You conducted a study with System Monitor. The processor on your Windows 2000 server is causing a bottleneck on your network. After adding more RAM, the problem still exists. What can you do?

    a. Add more RAM.

    b. Add additional hard drives.

    c. Upgrade to a faster processor.

    d. Add an additional processor to the dual-processor system board.

LAB 14.5 ESTABLISH A BASELINE

Objectives

The goal of this lab is to establish a baseline for your servers. As a network administrator, you will determine the level of system performance that you consider acceptable.

The baseline is established when your system is handling a typical workload and running all required services. The baseline performance is a subjective standard that you determine based on the work environment. You will configure performance logs to report data for the recommended counters at regular intervals, such as every 10 to 15 minutes. The baseline can be the measure used for setting performance expectations for your users.

Periodically, you will analyze future performance data against the baseline. Analyzing your monitoring data consists of examining counter values that are reported while your system performs various operations. During this process, you should determine which counters are most active, and compare these counters to the baseline. Using this type of performance data analysis, you can understand how your system responds to workload demands.

As a result of this analysis, you may find that your system performs satisfactorily at some times and unsatisfactorily at others. Depending on the causes of these variations and the degree of variance, you may choose to take corrective action, or to accept these variations. After completing this lab, you will be able to:

➤ Create a baseline log

➤ Load a baseline log into System Monitor

Materials Required

This lab will require the following:

➤ Access to a computer running Windows 2000 Member Server

➤ Completion of Labs 14.1 through 14.4

Estimated completion time: **15 minutes**

ACTIVITY

1. You should be logged on as administrator. Expand **Performance Logs and Alerts**, and then click **Counter Logs**.

2. Right-click in the right pane, click **New Log Settings**, type **Log*FML*** (where *F* is your first initial, *M* is your middle initial, and *L* is your last initial) in the **Name** text box , click **OK**, click the **General** tab, and then click **Add**.

Create the performance logs for input to a spreadsheet program. On the Log Files tab, click the Log file type drop-down list, and then click Text File - CSV.

3. Click the **Use local computer counters** option button, and then click the **Performance object** drop-down list. Scroll to find and then click **Processor**. Scroll to find and then click **% Processor Time**, click **_Total**, and then click **Add**.

4. Click the **Performance object** drop-down list. Scroll to find and then click **Memory**. Scroll to find and then click **Pages/sec**, and then click **Add**.

5. Click the **Performance object** drop-down list. Scroll to find and then click **PhysicalDisk.** Scroll to find and then click **% Disk Time**, click **0 C:** (your display may differ), click **Add**, click **Close**, and then click **Apply**.

You should click Yes if you see this message: Folder 'c:\PertfLogs', specified for the folder log folder, was not found....

6. Change the Sample data every: Interval text box to **5**, and then click **Apply**.

7. Click the **Schedule** tab, click **Start log Manually (using the shortcut menu)**, click **Apply**, and then click **OK**.

A green log icon indicates that the log is running, and a red icon indicates that it stopped.

8. Right-click **Log*FML***, and then click **Start**. Wait five minutes. Right-click **Log*FML***, and then click **Stop**.

9. Click **System Monitor**, and then click the **View Log File Data** button. Your screen should resemble Figure 14-5. Click **Log*FML*_*nnnnnn*.blg** (where *nnnnnn* is a sequence number supplied by Performance Logs and Alerts), and then click **Open**.

14

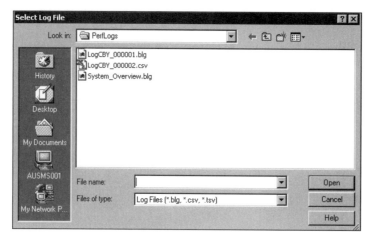

Figure 14-5 Select log file

 If the Log*FML_nnnnnn.blg* does not appear, click the Look in drop-down list, click C:, double-click PerfLogs, click Log*FML_nnnnnn.blg*, and then click Open.

10. Click the **Add Counter** button to open the Add Counters dialog box, and then click the **Use local computer counters** option button.

11. Click the **Performance object** drop-down list. Scroll to find and then click **Memory**, click the **All counters** option button, and then click **Add**.

12. Click the **Performance object** drop-down list. Scroll to find and then click **PhysicalDisk**, click the **All counters** option button, and then click **Add**.

13. Click the **Performance object** drop-down list. Scroll to find and then click **Processor**, click the **All counters** option button, click **Add**, and then click **Close**.

14. Observe your baseline graph. It reflects the activity of your server during normal conditions. You should be pleased that the lines are flat!

15. Remain logged on for the next lab.

Certification Objectives

Objectives Microsoft Exam 70-215: Installing, Configuring, and Administering Microsoft Windows 2000 Server:

➤ Monitor and optimize use of system resources

➤ Manage processes

➤ Optimize disk performance

➤ Manage and optimize availability of system and user data

Review Questions

1. You will discuss the best method to establish baseline performance data with your peers. Which of the following would be the best strategy?
   a. Capture System Monitor counters during non-peak periods throughout the day.
   b. Capture System Monitor counters during peak periods throughout the day.
   c. Capture System Monitor counters at regular intervals throughout the day.
   d. Capture Network Monitor information at peak periods throughout the day.

LAB 14.6 EXAMINE PROCESSOR ALERT

Objectives

The goal of this lab is to examine a processor usage alert on your server. An alert notification is sent by means of the messenger service when a predefined counter reaches, falls below, or rises above a defined threshold. As a network administrator, you can create an alert to send you a message when your server exceeds a predefined value. After completing this lab, you will be able to:

➤ Create a performance alert

➤ Add the % Processor counter

➤ Simulate various kinds of activity

➤ Respond to an alert message

Materials Required

This lab will require the following:

➤ Access to a computer running Windows 2000 Member Server

➤ Completion of Labs 14.1 through 14.4

➤ A value for the processor percentage

14

Estimated completion time: **15 minutes**

ACTIVITY

1. You should be logged on as administrator with the Performance window open.

2. Expand **Performance Logs and Alerts**, right-click **Alerts**, click **New Alert Settings…**, type **AlertFML** (where *F* is your first initial, *M* is your middle initial, and *L* is the initial of your last name) in the Name text box, and then click **OK**.

3. Type a **comment** in the Comment text box, press the **Tab** key, click the **Add** button, an then click the **Performance object** drop-down list. Scroll to find and then click **Processor**. Scroll to find and then click **% Processor Time**, click **_Total**, click **Add**, and then click **Close**. Your screen should resemble Figure 14-6.

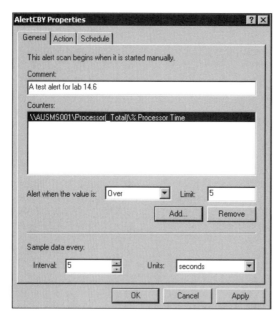

Figure 14-6   Creating an alert

4. Click the **Alert when the value is** drop-down list, click **Over**, press the **Tab** key, type *Percentage* (where *Percentage* is the value provided by your instructor) in the Limit text box, type **5** in the Interval text box, click the **Units** drop-down list, and then click **seconds**.

5. Click the **Action** tab, click the **Send a network message to** check box, type *server* (where *server* is the name for your member server) in the Send a message to text box, click **Apply**, and then click **OK**.

6. Move the **Performance** window to simulate activity, read the alert message, and then click **OK** for each alert message.

7. To cancel the alert, right-click **AlertFML**, and then click **Stop.**

8. Close the **Performance** window, click **No** to resulting message, and then log off.

Certification Objectives

Objectives Microsoft Exam 70-215: Installing, Configuring, and Administering Microsoft Windows 2000 Server:

➤ Monitor and optimize use of system resources

➤ Manage processes

➤ Manage and optimize availability of system and user data

Review Questions

1. Bob is reviewing Performance Logs and Alerts. He asks you about the various actions that can be taken when a performance counter rises above a threshold. Which of the following actions will you include in your discussion with Bob?

   a. Log an entry in the event log.

   b. Send an e-mail message to the system administrator.

   c. Run a program.

   d. Stop a system process.

14

CHAPTER FIFTEEN

NETWORK MONITORING AND TUNING

Labs included in this chapter

➤ Lab 15.1 Install Network Monitor and Driver

➤ Lab 15.2 Capturing Frames with Network Monitor

➤ Lab 15.3 Setting up Capture Filters

➤ Lab 15.4 Interpreting Captured Frames

➤ Lab 15.5 Monitoring a Network Interface and Server Activity with System Monitor

---

Microsoft MCSE Exam #70-215 Objectives	
Objective	Lab
Monitor and optimize usage of system resources	15.1, 15.2, 15.3, 15.4, 15.5
Install, configure, and troubleshoot network protocols	15.1, 15.2, 15.3, 15.4
Install and configure network services	15.2, 15.4, 15.3, 15.4, 15.5
Install, configure, and troubleshoot network adapters and drivers	15.2, 15.4, 15.3, 15.4, 15.5

LAB 15.1 INSTALL NETWORK MONITOR AND DRIVER

Objectives

The goal of this lab is to install Network Monitor and Network Monitor Driver. You will use Network Monitor to capture and display the frames (also called packets) that a computer running Windows 2000 Server receives from your Local Area Network (LAN). Network Monitor Driver can be installed only on computers running Microsoft Windows 2000 Professional or Windows 2000 Server.

As a network administrator, a working knowledge of the Windows 2000 network protocols is essential. For instance, you can use them to detect and troubleshoot networking problems that your local server might experience. You also might use Network Monitor to diagnose hardware and software problems when the server computer cannot communicate with other computers.

Network Monitor is the tool of choice to gain knowledge of the Windows 2000 network protocols. After starting Network Monitor to capture frames, you can complete a series of steps and review the captured frames. Network Monitor will decode the packets and provide the information to relate network activity to specific frames. After completing this lab, you will be able to:

➤ Install Network Monitor Driver

➤ Install Network Monitor

➤ Launch Network Monitor

➤ Select a Network Interface Card (NIC)

➤ Locate the four Network Monitor panes (Graph, Total Statistics, Session Statistics, and Station Statistics)

Materials Required

This lab will the following:

➤ Access to a computer running Windows 2000 Server

➤ A Windows 2000 Server CD-ROM

Estimated completion time: **15 minutes**

ACTIVITY

1. Log on as an **administrator**.

2. Click **Start**, point to **Settings**, click **Network and Dial-up Connections**, right-click **Local Area Connection**, and then click **Properties**.

3. Scroll and locate **Network Monitor Driver** in the scroll list. If Network Monitor Driver exists, click **Cancel**, close the **Network and Dial-up Connections** window, and then continue with Step 5. If Network Monitor Driver does not exist, go to Step 4.

4. Click **Install**, click **Protocol**, click **Add**, click **Network Monitor Driver**, click **OK**, and then click **Close**.

 If you are prompted for additional files, insert your Windows 2000 CD-ROM into the correct drive. If the CD-ROM autoruns, however, be sure to click Exit.

5. Click **Start**, point to **Settings**, click **Control Panel**, double-click **Add/Remove Programs**, click **Add/Remove Windows Components**, click the **Management and Monitoring Tools** check box, and then click **Details**.

6. Click to check the **Network Monitor Tools** check box, click **OK**, click **Next**, click **Next**, click **Finish**, click **Close**, and then close the **Control Panel** window.

 If you are prompted for additional files, insert your Windows 2000 CD-ROM into the correct drive. If the CD-ROM autoruns, however, be sure to click Exit.

7. Click **Start**, point to **Programs**, point to **Administrative Tools**, and then click **Network Monitor**. If you receive a message asking you to specify the network, click **OK**, and then continue with Step 9.

8. Click **Capture** on the menu bar, and then click **Networks**.

9. Expand **Local Computer**, and then click the first adapter.

10. Scroll to locate and then click **Dial-up Connection** in the right pane. If its value is TRUE, you have a modem connection. If it is FALSE, you have a NIC.

11. Repeat Step 10 until you locate the NIC. Then, click **OK**.

12. To learn the names of the network monitor panes, point to the **Toggle Graph Pane** button (third button on the toolbar), read the description, click the **Toggle Graph Pane** button, observe which pane is removed, click the **Toggle Graph Pane** button again, and then observe which pane returns.

 As you point to each button on the toolbar, an explanation for it appears on the status bar.

13. Repeat Step 12 for the Total Statistics Pane, the Session Statistics Pane, and the Station Statistics Pane. Leave all panes open for the next step.

14. Click **Tools** on the menu bar, click **Identify Network Monitor users**, click **Add Names to Address Database**, and then click **OK**.

15. Remove the CD-ROM, if used, and remain logged on with Microsoft Network Monitor open.

Certification Objectives

Objectives for Microsoft Exam 70-215: Installing, Configuring, and Administering Microsoft Windows 2000 Server:

➤ Monitor and optimize use of system resources

➤ Install, configure, and troubleshoot network protocols

➤ Install and configure network services

➤ Install, configure, and troubleshoot network adapters and drivers

Review Questions

1. You want to become more familiar with Network Monitor. Based upon your observations of Network Monitor, you complete a short list of the information that it displays. Which items will appear on your list?

   a. % network utilization

   b. network statistics

   c. network addresses of connected computers

   d. count of frames transmitted between connected computers

   e. number of broadcast frames

LAB 15.2 CAPTURING FRAMES WITH NETWORK MONITOR

Objectives

The objective of this lab is to capture network frames, which is important because network administrators are called upon to analyze network traffic. In this lab, you will capture all network traffic to and from the local network card. Network Monitor uses a Network Drive Interface Specification (NDIS) feature to copy all the frames it detects to its capture buffer After completing this lab, you will be able to:

➤ Locate the Start, Pause/Continue, and Stop Capture buttons

➤ Start a capture

➤ Create network activity with ping

➤ Stop a capture

Materials Required

This lab will require the following:

➤ Access to a computer running Windows 2000 Server with Network Monitor and Network Monitor Driver installed.

➤ Completion of Lab 15.1

➤ Name of a server (referred to as *server2* in this lab) from your instructor to test a connection with the ping command.

Estimated completion time: **15 minutes**

ACTIVITY

1. You should be logged on with Microsoft Network Monitor open. Point to the **Start Capture** button (ninth button on the toolbar). Read the explanation shown on the status bar at the bottom of window.

2. Repeat Step 1 for the Pause/Continue Capture and Stop Capture buttons.

3. Click the **Start Capture** button.

4. Click **Start**, point to **Programs**, point to **Accessories**, click **Command Prompt**, type **Ping *server2*** (where *server2* is the computer name provided by your instructor), and then press **Enter**. Minimize the **Command Prompt** window.

5. Return to the **Microsoft Network Monitor** window, and then click the **Stop Capture** button. Your screen should resemble Figure 15-1.

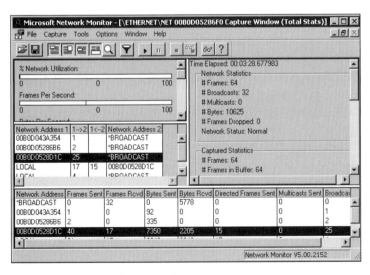

Figure 15-1   Sample network capture

6. Remain logged on with the Microsoft Network Monitor window open and the Command Prompt window minimized.

Certification Objectives

Objectives for Microsoft Exam 70-215: Installing, Configuring, and Administering Microsoft Windows 2000 Server:

➤ Monitor and optimize use of system resources

➤ Install, configure, and troubleshoot network protocols

➤ Install and configure network services

➤ Install, configure, and troubleshoot network adapters and drivers

Review Questions

1. Indicate the correct sequence of steps to capture a series of frames created by a simple network activity.

   1. Install a network packet trapper card.
   2. Launch Network Monitor.
   3. Start the network activity.
   4. Start the capture.
   5. Stop the capture.
   6. View the capture summary.
   7. Export the captured frames to a protocol analyzer program.
   a. 1, 2, 4, 3, 5, 6
   b. 2, 4, 3, 5, 6
   c. 1, 4, 3, 5, 7
   d. 1, 4, 3, 5, 7
   e. 2, 3, 4, 5, 6

2. You are designing a network study to resolve the problems that occur between the Windows 2000 database application servers and the client computers. You establish the following goals for your study:

   1. Capture frames on the database server
   2. Capture frames on the Windows 2000 Professional client computers
   3. Capture frames on the Windows 98 client computers
   4. Interpret the captured frames

   To achieve your goals, you will install Network Monitor and Network Monitor Driver on the Windows 2000 database application server that will be used to monitor the transmitted frames. You will install Network Driver on three representative Windows 2000 Professional client computers. You will then install Network Monitor Driver on three representative Windows 98 client computers.

At a predetermined time, users at the six representative client computers will start the client application to access the Windows 2000 database application server. Regarding your efforts, which of the following statements is correct?

a. Goal 1 will be met.

b. Goal 2 will be met.

c. Goal 3 will be met.

d. Goal 4 will be met.

e. No goals will be met.

LAB 15.3 SETTING UP CAPTURE FILTERS

Objectives

The objective of this lab is to set up a capture filter to specify the types of network information you want to monitor. For example, to see only a specific subset of computers or protocols, you can specify the computers and protocols in a capture filter.

By filtering frames, you save both buffer resources and time. To design a display filter, you specify decision statements in the Capture Filter dialog box. This dialog box displays the filter's decision tree, which is a graphical representation of your filter's logic. When you include or exclude information from your capture specifications, the decision tree reflects those specifications. After completing this lab, you will be able to:

➤ Open the Capture Filter dialog box

➤ Build an address expression for one address to many addresses

➤ Save a capture filter

Materials Required

This lab will require the following:

➤ Access to a computer running Windows 2000 Server

➤ Completion of Labs 15.1 and 15.2.

➤ Name of a server (referred to as *server2* in this lab) from your instruction to ping.

15

Estimated completion time: **15 minutes**

ACTIVITY

1. You should be logged on with the Microsoft Network Monitor window open and the Command Prompt window minimized. Click **Capture** on the menu bar, click **Filter**, and then click **OK** to the resultant message box.

2. Click **(Address Pairs)**, as shown in Figure 15-2.

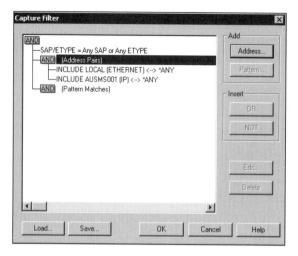

Figure 15-2   Completed capture filter

3. Click the **Address** button, click *server1* (where *server1* is the name of your server) in the Station 1 pane, and then click **OK**. Your screen should resemble Figure 15–3.

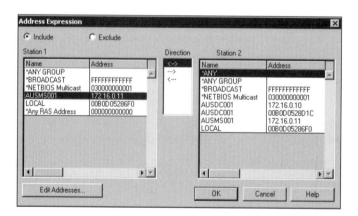

Figure 15-3   Building an address expression

4. Click the **Address** button, click **LOCAL** in the Station 1 pane, and then click **OK**.

5. Click **Save**, type **Cap*FML*** (where *F* is your first initial, *M* is your middle initial, and *L* is your last initial) in the File name text box, click **Save**, and then click **OK**

6. Click the **Start Capture** button. If the Do you want to save the capture? message appears, click **No**.

7. Return to the **Command Prompt** window, type **Ping** *server2* (where *server2* is the name provided by your instructor), and then press **Enter**. Minimize the **Command Prompt** window.

8. Return to the **Network Monitor** window, and then click the **Stop Capture** button.

9. Remain logged on with the Network Monitor window open for the next lab.

Certification Objectives

Objectives for Microsoft Exam 70-215: Installing, Configuring, and Administering Microsoft Windows 2000 Server:

➤ Monitor and optimize use of system resources

➤ Install, configure, and troubleshoot network protocols

➤ Install and configure network services

➤ Install, configure, and troubleshoot network adapters and drivers

Review Questions

1. George is developing a procedure for network administrators to use when creating filters for Network Monitor. Which answer indicates the correct sequence of steps?

    1. Access the Capture menu.
    2. Access the Capture Filter dialog box from the Filters menu.
    3. Click Add Address.
    4. Access (Address Pairs).
    5. Select your computer as Station 1.
    6. Select the another computer as Station 2.
    7. Click OK to enter the Address Expression.

    a. 1, 2, 4, 3, 5, 6, 7

    b. 2, 3, 4, 5, 6, 7

    c. 1, 2, 3, 4, 5, 6, 7

    d. 1, 2, 3, 5, 6, 7

15

LAB 15.4 INTERPRETING CAPTURED FRAMES

Objectives

The objective of this lab is to interpret the frames captured in the previous lab. As a network administrator, you will use captured data to discover the contents of frames on your network. Fortunately, Network Monitor does much of the data analysis for you by translating the raw captured data into its logical frame structure.

Frames, whether broadcast or directed, are made up of several different pieces that can be analyzed separately. Some of these pieces contain data that you can use to troubleshoot networking problems. For example, by examining the destination address, you can determine whether the frame was a broadcast frame, which indicates all hosts had to receive and process this frame, or a directed frame that was sent to a specific host. By analyzing frames, you can determine the exact cause of the frame, which helps you understand the network activity for your network.

The Frame Viewer window includes the following panes:

> Summary, which provides general information about captured frames in the order in which they were captured

> Detail, which provides the frame's contents, including the protocols used to send

> Hex, which is a hexadecimal and ASCII representation of the captured data

After completing this lab, you will be able to:

> Display the capture data summary

> Select a frame for study

> Review the contents of captured data frames

Materials Required

This lab will require the following:

Access to a computer running Windows 2000 Server

Completion of Labs 15.1 through 15.3

Estimated completion time: **15 minutes**

ACTIVITY

1. You should be logged on with the Network Monitor window open to the capture from Lab 15.3. Click **Capture** on the menu bar, and then click **Display Captured Data**. Your screen should resemble Figure 15-4.

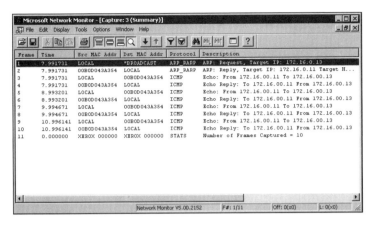

Figure 15-4   Captured summary

 The process for displaying captured frames is the same for all servers. However, your frames will reflect the dynamic nature of network traffic. For your capture, the protocol for your first line could be a DNS request, an ARP request, or an ICMP Echo.

2. Double-click the first line in the captured data summary. Your screen should resemble Figure 15-5.

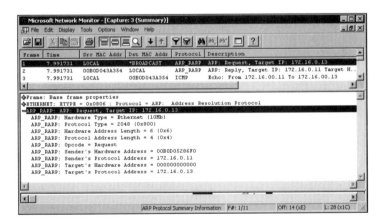

Figure 15-5   Sample frame detail

15

 To see more of the analysis pane (the middle pane), drag its bottom bar. To review the detail, scroll in the analysis pane (middle pane). Locate the last gold +, double-click the gold + to expand the frame analysis, and then scroll to read the explanation.

3. Click the next line in the top pane to display the next frame. Expand the frame for additional detail.

4. Repeat Step 3 for the remaining frames that were captured.

5. Close the Network Monitor window, click **No** to the Do you want to save the capture? message, and then click **No** to the You have unsaved entries in your address database message.

6. Remain logged on for the next lab.

Certification Objectives

Objectives for Microsoft Exam 70-215: Installing, Configuring, and Administering Microsoft Windows 2000 Server:

➤ Monitor and optimize use of system resources

➤ Install, configure, and troubleshoot network protocols

➤ Install and configure network services

➤ Install, configure, and troubleshoot network adapters and drivers

Review Questions

1. Brian and Lillie discuss the information that is available in the capture summary. You are asked to provide a list of the items. Which items will be included in your list?
   a. frame number
   b. elapsed time between frames
   c. source NIC address
   d. destination NIC address
   e. protocol type
   f. description of packet

2. At your weekly network administrators meeting, you are asked to present a brief overview of Network Monitor. Which items will be included in your overview?
   a. You can install Network Monitor only on computers that have Windows 2000 installed.
   b. You can add Network Monitor Driver on a variety of Windows products, including Windows ME, Windows NT, and Windows 2000.
   c. With Windows 2000 Network Monitor, you can view all frames over the network.
   d. By using Capture Filter, you can exclude broadcast frames from your capture.
   e. You can view the decoded frame content for each captured frame.

LAB 15.5 MONITORING A NETWORK INTERFACE AND SERVER ACTIVITY WITH SYSTEM MONITOR

Objectives

The objective of this lab is to utilize System Monitor with network objects. Network monitoring typically consists of observing server resource utilization and measuring overall network traffic. Administrators commonly perform this activity so that they can observe changes in network activity. You can start the process by tracking the counters that monitor the bytes sent and received over your NIC. To measure server activity, you can use the total bytes processed by the server. After completing this lab, you will be able to:

➤ Launch System Monitor

➤ Add network counters to the network object

➤ Add a counter to the server object

➤ Simulate network activity

➤ Review the results using System Monitor

Materials Required

This lab will require the following:

➤ Access to a computer running Windows 2000 Server

➤ Name of a server (referred to as *server3* in this lab) from your instructor, and a folder (referred to as *folder3* in this lab) to access from a second computer.

Estimated completion time: **15 minutes**

15

ACTIVITY

1. You should be logged on to your computer. Click **Start**, point to **Programs**, point to **Administrative Tools**, and then click **Performance**.

2. Click **System Monitor**, and then click the **Add Counter** button to open the Add Counters dialog box.

3. Click the **Performance object** drop-down list. Scroll to find and then click **Network Interface**. Scroll to find and then click **Bytes Received/sec** from the select counter list. Click *NetworkInterfaceCard* from the select instances list (where *NetworkInterfaceCard* is the card installed on your server), click **Explain**, read the explanation for the counter, and then click **Add**.

4. Scroll to find and then click **Bytes Sent/sec**, click *NetworkInterfaceCard*, read the explanation for the counter, and then click **Add**.

5. Click the **Performance object** drop-down list. Scroll to find and then click **Server**. Scroll to find and then click **Bytes Total/sec**, read the explanation for the counter, click **Add**, and then click **Close**.

6. Click **Start**, point to **Search**, click **For Files or Folders**, type **lonestar** in the Containing text text box, click the **Look in** drop-down list, click **Browse**, expand **My Network Places**, expand **Entire Network**, expand **Microsoft Windows Network**, expand **Lonestar**, expand *server3* (where *server3* is the server name provided by your instructor), click *folder3* (where *folder3* is the folder name provided by your instructor), and then click **OK**.

7. Click **Search Now**, minimize the **Search Results** window, and then observe the changes in the counters.

8. Maximize the **Search Results** window, click **Stop Search**, and then close the **Search Results** window.

9. Close the **Performance** window, close any open applications, and then log off the computer.

Certification Objectives

Objectives for Microsoft Exam 70-215: Installing, Configuring, and Administering Microsoft Windows 2000 Server:

➤ Monitor and optimize use of system resources

➤ Install, configure, and troubleshoot network protocols

➤ Install and configure network services

➤ Install, configure, and troubleshoot network adapters and drivers

Review Questions

1. Phil considers monitoring a Windows 2000 file and print server. He wants to include counters that will measure network performance and possible indications of problems with a server's processor, memory, or hard disks. Which of the following counters should Phil implement?

   a. Memory\Pages/sec

   b. Processor\ % Processor Time

   c. Memory\Available Bytes

   d. PhysicalDisk\% Disk Time

   e. Network\Bytes Sent/sec

   f. Network\Bytes Received/sec

CHAPTER SIXTEEN

TROUBLESHOOTING

Labs included in this chapter

➤ Lab 16.1 Monitor an Adjacent Computer
➤ Lab 16.2 Troubleshoot TCP/IP Connectivity
➤ Lab 16.3 Booting in Safe Mode
➤ Lab 16.4 Installing and Using the Recovery Console
➤ Lab 16.5 Using the Security Configuration and Analysis Snap-in Objective

Microsoft MCSE Exam #70-215 Objectives	
Objective	**Lab**
Install and configure network services for interoperability	16.2
Configure hardware devices	16.3, 16.4
Troubleshoot problems with hardware	16.2, 16.3, 16.4
Monitor and optimize usage of system resources	16.1
Optimize disk performance	16.1
Recover systems and user data	16.3, 16.4
Monitor, configure, and troubleshoot disks and volumes	16.4
Recover from disk failures	16.4
Install and configure network services	16.2
Install, configure, and troubleshoot network adapters and drivers	16.2
Implement, configure, manage, and troubleshoot policies in a Windows 2000 environment	16.5
Implement, configure, manage, and troubleshoot local accounts	16.5
Implement, configure, manage, and troubleshoot Account Policy	16.5
Implement, configure, manage, and troubleshoot security by using the Security Configuration Tool Set	16.5

LAB 16.1 MONITOR AN ADJACENT COMPUTER

Objectives

The objective of this lab is to use Computer Management to monitor the status of a adjacent or remote computer. With Computer Management, you can manage remote computers using a single, consolidated desktop tool. With this technology, you can set up management consoles for the various servers on your network and manage them from single computer. After completing this lab, you will be able to:

➤ Create a management console for a server on the network

➤ View the event log on the remote server

➤ Create a filter for an event log

➤ Review device status on a remote computer

➤ Start a service on a remote computer

Materials Required

This lab will require the following:

➤ Access to a computer running Windows 2000 Server

➤ Instructor-provided server name for the server that you will manage. This server refereed to as *server1* in this lab.

Estimated completion time: **15 minutes**

ACTIVITY

1. Log on as an **administrator**.

2. Click **Start**, click **Run**, type **MMC**, and then click **OK**.

3. Click **Console**, click **Add/Remove Snap-in**, click **Add**, click **Computer Management**, click **Add**, click **Another computer**, and then click **Browse**. Your screen should resemble Figure 16-1.

You may get a message when you connect to a remote computer. Click OK if you see that message.

4. Click *server1* (where *server1* is the name supplied by your instructor), click **OK**, click **Finish**, click **Close**, click **OK**, expand **computer Management**, expand **System Tools**, and then expand **Event Viewer**.

5. Click **Application**, view the application log, click the **View** menu, click **Filter**, uncheck the **Information** check box, click **Apply**, and then click **OK**.

6. Repeat Step 5 for the Security and System logs.

7. Expand **System Information**, click **System Summary**, and then review the system summary information in the right pane.

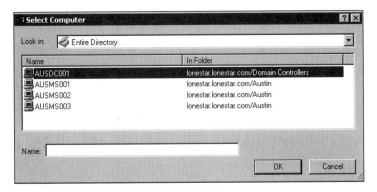

Figure 16-1   Select computer to manage

8. Repeat Step 7 for remaining items under System Information.

9. Click **Device Manager**, and then click **OK** to the Device Manager is running in read-only mode... message. Expand **Network adapters**, right-click **installed adapter**, click **Properties**, click the **General** tab, and then review the contents of the Review dialog box.

10. Click the **Driver** tab, review the contents of the dialog box, click the **Resources** tab, review the contents of the dialog box, and then click **OK**.

11. Expand **Storage**, and then click **Disk Management**. In the upper-right pane, scroll to read **Free Space**.

12. Expand **Services and Applications**, click **Services**, and then scroll to find and right-click the **Telnet** service in the right pane. Click **Properties**, click the **General** tab, review the contents of the dialog box, and then locate the **Service status**, as shown in Figure 16-2 on the next page.

13. If the Service status is stopped, click **Start**, wait for service to start, and then click **OK**. Otherwise, click **Stop**, wait for the service to stop, click **Start**, and then click **OK**.

14. Close the **Microsoft Management Console** window, and then click **No** to the Save Console settings... message.

15. Remain logged on for the next lab.

16

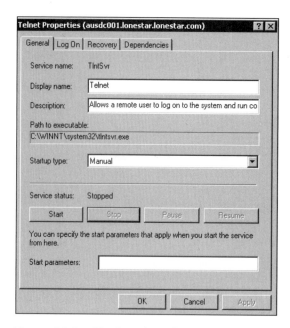

Figure 16-2   Starting the Telnet service

Certification Objectives

Objectives for Microsoft Exam 70-215: Installing, Configuring, and Administering Microsoft Windows 2000 Server:

➤ Monitor and optimize use of system resources

➤ Manage and optimize availability of system and user data

➤ Install, configure, and troubleshoot shared access

➤ Install, configure, and troubleshoot network protocols

Review Questions

1. You are asked to provide your peer group with a brief presentation on monitoring computers over the network. Which items will be included in your presentation?

   a. discussion of viewing the system log on a remote computer with Event Viewer

   b. discussion of viewing the volumes and free space on a remote computer

   c. discussion of starting and stopping services

   d. discussion of changing IRQs on remote devices with Device Manager

   e. discussion of managing multiple computers with the same console

2. What is the correct sequence of the following steps to start the Telnet service when it stops?

a. Open the Microsoft Management Console (MMC) where the Computer Management snap-in was previously installed.

b. Click Services.

c. Expand Services and Applications.

d. Click the Telnet service.

e. Click Properties.

f. Wait for the Telnet service to start.

g. Click Start.

h. Click OK.

    1. 1, 3, 2, 5, 4, 7, 6, 8

    2. 1, 3, 2, 4, 5, 7, 6, 8

    3. 1, 2, 3, 4, 5, 7, 6, 8

    4. 1, 2, 3, 4, 5, 6, 7, 8

LAB 16.2 TROUBLESHOOT TCP/IP CONNECTIVITY

Objectives

The objective of this lab is to use common TCP/IP utilities to troubleshoot network connectivity. As a network administrator, you must troubleshoot failed connections with these tools. You can use the PING utility to determine if the TCP/IP software was installed and configured properly. In addition, you will find NETVIEW useful for determining the names of available servers.

Another useful tool is NBTSTAT for troubleshooting NetBIOS name resolution problems. You can display the names that were registered locally on the system by programs, such as the server and redirector. In addition, you can obtain a list of the current NetBIOS sessions and their status, including statistics.

NETSTAT is a particularly helpful tool. It displays IP protocol statistics and current TCP/IP network connections. You can display per-protocol statistics with the -s option. With the -p option, you can specify a specific protocol, and with the -a option, you can display the active connections. After completing this lab, you will be able to:

16

➤ Determine if TCP/IP is installed properly

➤ Determine if the computername can be resolved

➤ Determine the computername registered on the network

➤ Determine the NetBIOS name table

➤ Determine the NetBIOS connections

➤ Determine the TCP/IP statistics

➤ Determine the TCP/IP connections

Materials Required

This lab will the following:

➤ Access to a computer running Windows 2000 Server

Estimated completion time: **15 minutes**

ACTIVITY

1. You should be logged on to your computer. Click **Start**, point to **Programs**, point to **Accessories**, and then click **Command Prompt**.

2. Type **ping 127.0.0.1**, and then press **Enter**.

If TCP/IP is installed properly, you will see Reply from 127.0.0.1.... Otherwise, you will see a message similar to Unable to connect IP driver....

3. Type **net use \\\unknown\unknown** (where \\\unknown\unknown is the name of a nonexistent computer and share on your network), and then press **Enter**. You should see the following message: System error 53 has occurred. The network path was not found. This error indicates that the computername "unknown" could not be resolved.

4. You will now determine the correct server names. Type **net view**, and then press. **Enter** to produce a list of the computernames on your network.

5. Type **nbtstat**, and then press **Enter** to display the switches for NBTSTAT.

6. Type **nbtstat –n**, and then press **Enter** to display the NetBIOS local name table.

7. Type **nbtstat –s**, and then press **Enter** to display the NetBIOS connection table.

You can add "| more" to most commands submitted to the Command Prompt. This will pause the display. Once the display is paused, you can press the space-bar for the next portion of the text.

8. Type **netstat /? | more**, and then press **Enter** to display the switches for NETSTAT.

9. Type **netstat –s**, and then press **Enter** to display statistics.

10. Type **netstat –a –p tcp**, and then press **Enter** to display TCP connections.

11. Type **exit**, and then press **Enter**. Remain logged on for the next lab.

Certification Objectives

Objectives for Microsoft Exam 70-215: Installing, Configuring, and Administering Microsoft Windows 2000 Server:

➤ Monitor and optimize use of system resources

➤ Manage and optimize availability of system and user data

➤ Install, configure, and troubleshoot shared access

➤ Install, configure, and troubleshoot network protocols

Review Questions

1. You need to display protocol statistics and the state of current TCP/IP connections on a Windows 2000 server. Which command line utility will you use?
   a. NBTSTAT
   b. NETSTAT
   c. TCPSTAT
   d. IPCONFIG

2. You need to display protocol statistics and the state of current NetBIOS connections on a Windows 2000 server. Which command line utility will you use?
   a. NBTSTAT
   b. NETSTAT
   c. TCPSTAT
   d. IPCONFIG

3. You need to determine the computernames for the servers on your network. Which command line utility will you use?
   a. NET SERVERS
   b. NET USE
   c. NET COMPUTERS
   d. NET VIEW
   e. NET SHARES

16

Lab 16.3 Boot in Safe Mode

Objectives

The goal of this lab is to boot a server in Safe Mode. You can use Safe Mode to diagnos: problems. If a symptom does not reappear when you start in Safe Mode, you can eliminat: the default settings and minimum device drivers as possible causes. If a newly added devic: or a changed driver is causing problems, you can use Safe Mode to remove the device c reverse the change.

In Safe Mode, Windows 2000 uses only basic files and drivers, such as the mouse, the mon itor, the keyboard, mass storage, the base video, and the default system services. It does n: use network connections. You can select the Safe Mode with the Command Prompt optio: This option is exactly the same as Safe Mode except that a Command Prompt window star: instead of Windows 2000.

In this lab, you will choose the Safe Mode with Networking option, which loads all c the above files and drivers, plus the essential services and drivers to start networkin; Then, you will restart the computer and choose Safe Mode with Command Promp: After completing this lab, you will be able to:

➤ Shutdown and restart a server

➤ Select Safe Mode with Networking

➤ Verify with Safe Mode with Networking that LAN connections exist

➤ Select Safe Mode with Command Prompt

Materials Required

This lab will require the following:

➤ Access to a computer running Windows 2000 Server

Estimated completion time: **15 minutes**

Activity

1. You should be logged on to your computer to begin this lab. Click **Start**, click **Shutdown**, click the **What do you want the computer to do?** drop-down list, click **Restart**, click **OK**, and then wait for the computer to shutdown.

2. When the **Starting Windows...** text appears on your screen, press **F8**.

3. Review the available options. Use the **arrow key** on your keyboard to move th: highlight to **Safe Mode with Networking,** and then press **Enter**. Wait for Windows 2000 to start in black-screen VGA Mode.

4. Log on to the server as **administrator**.

5. Read the message displayed in the window, and then click **OK**.

6. Click **Start**, point to **Settings**, click **Network and Dial-up Connections**, and then double-click **Local Area Connection**.

7. Verify the connection status, duration, and speed information in the Local Area Connection Status dialog box, click **Close**, and then close the **Network and DialUp Connections** dialog box.

8. Click **Start**, click **Shutdown**, and then click **OK** to restart the computer. Wait for the computer to shutdown.

9. When the Starting Windows... text appears on your screen, press **F8**.

10. Review the available options. Use the **arrow key** on your keyboard to move the highlight to **Safe Mode with Command Prompt**, and then press **Enter**. Wait for Windows to start in black-screen VGA Mode.

11. Log on as **administrator**, and then wait for the Command Prompt window.

12. Type **dir**, and then press **Enter**.

13. Type **net view**, and then press **Enter**. You should see The service has not been started message.

14. Type **exit**, and then press **Enter**.

15. Press **Ctrl-Alt-Del**, click **Shutdown**, and then click **OK** to restart the computer.

Certification Objectives

Objectives for Microsoft Exam 70-215: Installing, Configuring, and Administering Microsoft Windows 2000 Server:

➤ Monitor and optimize use of system resources

➤ Manage and optimize availability of system and user data

➤ Install, configure, and troubleshoot shared access

➤ Install, configure, and troubleshoot network protocols

➤ Update device drivers

16

Review Questions

1. You installed a new network adapter card on a Windows 2000 server. After installing the hardware and software, the system starts fine, but when Windows 2000 starts, you receive a message indicating that a dependent service did not start. Which step would you use to resolve the problem?

a. Restart the computer, press F8, and start in Safe Mode with Networking.

b. Restart the computer, press F8, and start in Safe Mode with Command Prompt.

       c. Restart the computer, press F8, and start in Safe Mode.

       d. Restart the computer.

  2. You experiment with the various Safe Mode alternatives. Then, you create a short list of the characteristics of the various alternatives. Which of the following items are on your list?

       a. If a newly added device or a changed driver is causing problems, you can use Safe Mode to remove the device or reverse the change.

       b. For Safe Mode, Windows 2000 uses only basic files and drivers.

       c. For Safe Mode, Windows 2000 only provides a Command Prompt window.

       d. For Safe Mode with Networking, networking starts.

       e. For Safe Mode with Networking, Windows 2000 provides the GUI interface.

LAB 16.4 INSTALL AND USE THE RECOVERY CONSOLE

Objectives

The goal of this lab is to install and investigate the Recovery Console. Using the Recovery Console, you can start and stop services, partition drives, fix boot sectors, read and write data on a local drive (including drives formatted to use NTFS), and perform many other administrative tasks. However, you cannot access the network. After completing this lab, you will be able to:

➤ Install the Recovery Console

➤ Review the Recovery Console commands

➤ Determine directory contents

➤ Review disk volumes

➤ Launch the disk partition program

Materials Required

This lab will require the following:

➤ Access to a computer running Windows 2000 Server

➤ A Windows 2000 Server CD-ROM

Estimated completion time: **15 minutes**

ACTIVITY

  1. Log on as an **administrator**.

  2. Insert the Windows 2000 Server CD-ROM, and then click **Exit** when the CD autoruns.

3. Click **Start**, click **Run**, type **<CD-ROM>\i386\winnt32 /cmdcons** (where *<CD-ROM>* is the drive letter for the CD-ROM), and then click **OK**.

4. Read the Windows 2000 Setup message, click **Yes**, and then wait for the Recovery Console to be installed.

5. Read the Microsoft Windows 2000 Advanced Server message, and then click **OK**.

6. Remove the CD-ROM from the drive.

7. Click **Start**, click **Shutdown**, click the **What do you want the computer to do?** drop-down list, click **Restart**, click **OK**, and then wait for the computer to shutdown.

Because the Recovery Console is quite powerful, it should only be used by network administrators who have a thorough knowledge of Windows 2000. If it is used carelessly, you run the risk of damaging your operating system beyond repair!

8. When the Please select operating system to start menu appears, use the **arrow keys** to move the highlight to **Microsoft Windows 2000 Recovery Console**, and then press **Enter**.

9. When the Windows 2000 Recovery Console menu appears, locate the **installation number** to log on to, type that number, and then press **Enter**.

10. Type the **administrator password**, and then press **Enter**.

11. Type **help**, and then press **Enter** to display a list of available commands. Press the **spacebar** until the help text returns to the Command Prompt window.

12. Type **dir**, press **Enter**, and then press **spacebar** until the directory listing returns to the Command Prompt.

13. Type **map**, and then press **Enter** to display the volume table.

14. Type **map arc**, and then press **Enter** to display the ARC paths.

15. Type **help fixboot**, and then press **Enter** to see the fixboot help.

16. Type **help fixmbr**. Press **Enter** to see fix master boot record help.

17. Type **help diskpart**, and then press **Enter** to see disk partition help.

18. Type **diskpart**, and then press **Enter** to see disk partitions. Press **Esc** to exit.

19. Type **listsvc**, and then press **Enter** to display status of services. Press the **spacebar** until the services listing returns to the Command Prompt.

20. Type **exit**, and then press **Enter** to restart the computer.

16

Certification Objectives

Objectives for Microsoft Exam 70-215: Installing, Configuring, and Administering Microsoft Windows 2000 Server:

➤ Monitor and optimize use of system resources

➤ Manage and optimize availability of system and user data

➤ Install, configure, and troubleshoot shared access

➤ Install, configure, and troubleshoot network protocols

➤ Update device drivers

Review Questions

1. You have read about Recovery Console. You engage George in a discussion about the command line programs in Recovery Console. George is skeptical. Which of the following items will you indicate that you can do with Recovery Console?
   a. Copy a file from a disk to the hard drive.
   b. Log on to the network with the LOGON command.
   c. Map to a shared folder on another Windows 2000 server with the MAP command.
   d. View and alter disk partitions with the DISKPART command.
   e. Edit the boot.ini file with the NOTEPAD command.

LAB 16.5 USE THE SECURITY CONFIGURATION AND ANALYSIS SNAP-IN

Objectives

The goal of this lab is to install and use the Security Configuration and Analysis tool. You will use the Security Configuration and Analysis tool for analyzing and configuring local system security. Administrators find this tool useful for auditing security on existing servers

With Security Configuration and Analysis, you can obtain a quick review of security Recommendations are presented alongside current system settings. You can then review the highlighted areas where the current settings do not match your proposed level of security At that time, you can resolve any discrepancies revealed by the analysis. After completing this lab, you will be able to:

➤ Install the Security Configuration and Analysis snap-in

➤ Select a security template for a proposed level of security

➤ Save the security database

➤ Analyze the security on your server

➤ Review the security differences between your server and the security template

➤ Resolve security differences for your server

Materials Required

This lab will require the following:

➤ Access to a computer running Windows 2000 Server

Estimated completion time: **15 minutes**

ACTIVITY

1. Log on as an **administrator**.

2. To install the Security and Configuration Analysis snap-in, click **Start**, click **Run**, type **MMC**, click **OK**, click **Console**, click **Add/Remove Snap-In**, click **Add**, click **Security Configuration and Analysis**, click **Add**, click **Close**, and then click **OK**.

3. To set up a security template, right-click **Security Configuration and Analysis**, click **Open database**, type **SecFML** (where F is your first initial, M is your second initial, and L is your last initial), click **Open**, click **basicsv.inf**, click **Clear this database before importing**, and then click **Open**.

4. Click **Security Configuration and Analysis** in the left pane, read the message in the right pane, and then record on a sheet of paper the location for the Security Database.

5. Right-click **Security Configuration and Analysis**, click **Analyze Computer Now**, review the location for the Error log file path, and then click **OK**.

6. Wait for the analysis to complete.

7. Expand **Security Configurations and Analysis**, click **System Services**, and then review the settings. Your screen should resemble Figure 16-3.

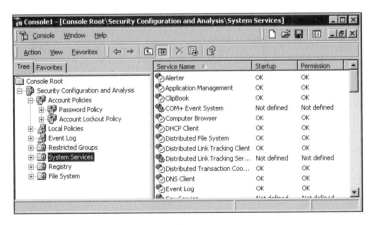

Figure 16-3   Security review for system services

16

In the right pane, three possible states exist: a red X indicates that settings disagree, a green check indicates agreement, and no mark indicates that the attribute was not configured in the security template.

8. Expand **Account Policies**, click **Password Policy**, and then review the password policies. Your screen should resemble Figure 16-4. If a red x exists on a policy, skip to Step 12. Otherwise, continue with Step 9.

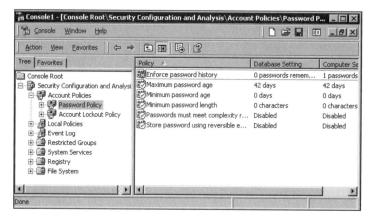

Figure 16-4   Security difference indicated

9. Expand **Local Policies**, click **Audit Policy**, and then review the audit policies. If a red x exists on a policy, skip to Step 12. Otherwise, continue with Step 10.

10. Expand **Local Policies**, click **User Rights Assignment**, and then review the audit policies. If a red x exists on a policy, skip to Step 12. Otherwise, continue with Step 11.

11. Click **Security Options**, and then review the audit policies. If a red x exists on a policy, continue with Step 12. (If you did not locate a red x for Steps 9 through 11, ask your instructor for assistance.)

12. Right-click any policy that was identified in Steps 9, 10, or 11, and then click **Security**.

13. Click the **Define this policy in the database** check box, if necessary, complete the policy as required by the dialog box, and then click **OK**. Your screen should resemble Figure 16-5.

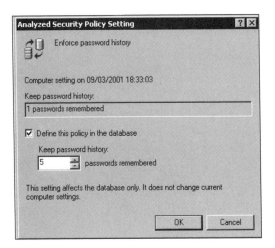

Figure 16-5   Policy reconciliation

14. Close the **Microsoft Management Console** window, and then click **No** to the Save console settings... message.

15. Click **Yes** to save the revised security template.

16. Log off the computer.

Certification Objectives

Objectives for Microsoft Exam 70-215: Installing, Configuring, and Administering Microsoft Windows 2000 Server:

➤ Monitor and optimize use of system resources

➤ Manage and optimize availability of system and user data

➤ Install, configure, and troubleshoot shared access

➤ Implement, configure, manage, and troubleshoot security by using the Security Configuration and Analysis tool

16

Review Questions

1. Brian and Lillie ask you about the Security Configuration and Analysis tool. Which of the following items would you discuss with Brian and Lillie?

a. You can use it for analyzing local system security against a security template.

b. You can use it to obtain a review of security.

c. It gives database settings alongside current system settings.

d. With it, you can resolve any revealed discrepancies for each security attribute.

2. Brian and Lillie have the MMC open with Security and Configuration displayed. They completed an analysis for the security on a server. They point out that there appear to be several states in the analysis window. Which items will you discuss with Brian and Lillie?

    a. A green check indicates agreement between the server and the security template.

    b. A red mark indicates agreement between the server and the security template

    c. A yellow mark indicates partial agreement between the server and the security template.

    d. No mark indicates that the security template does not have a matching attribute.